THE E-LEARNING
REVOLUTION

DATE DUE

GAYLORD   PRINTED IN U.S.A.

THE E-LEARNING REVOLUTION

How Technology Is Driving a New Training Paradigm

Martyn Sloman

American Management Association

New York • Atlanta • Brussels • Buenos Aires • Chicago • London • Mexico City
San Francisco • Shanghai • Tokyo • Toronto • Washington, D.C.

Special discounts on bulk quantities of AMACOM books are available to corporations, professional associations, and other organizations. For details, contact Special Sales Department, AMACOM, a division of American Management Association, 1601 Broadway, New York, NY 10019.
Tel.: 212-903-8316.   Fax: 212-903-8083.
Web site: www.amacombooks.org

This publication is designed to provide accurate and authoritative information in regard to the subject matter covered. It is sold with the understanding that the publisher is not engaged in rendering legal, accounting, or other professional service. If legal advice or other expert assistance is required, the services of a competent professional person should be sought.

Library of Congress Cataloging-in-Publication Data

Sloman, Martyn.
    The e-learning revolution : how technology is driving a new training paradigm / Martyn Sloman.
        p.   cm.
    Includes bibliographical references and index.
    ISBN 0-8144-7155-2
    1. Employees—Training of—Data processing.   2. Organizational learning—Data processing.   3. Computer-assisted instruction.   I. Title.

HF5549.5.T7 S6198   2002
658.3'124'0285—dc21   2002004266

Printing number

10   9   8   7   6   5   4   3   2   1

For Seth and Dorothy Dubin in appreciation of their generosity to my family.

CONTENTS

LIST OF CASE STUDIES

PREFACE

This book is written from the point of view of a practicing human resources manager. I have been fortunate to have worked in the profession that I enjoy, and consider to be thoroughly worthwhile, for the past twenty years. Over the last decade, I have served as the head of a training function in several organizations. There have been numerous changes in that twenty-year period—most of them beneficial in that they have enabled human resources and corporate training to become more effective. New approaches to business strategy, with more emphasis on competition through people, is one example. The emergence and acceptance of competencies and the growing use of competency frameworks is another.

Nothing, however, approaches the gains to be won from the connected economy. This term, and its underlying elements, are explored and explained more fully in the chapters that follow. In essence, the interlinking of computers and the acceptance of communication protocols through the World Wide Web have created the Internet. This will force us to do our jobs in a totally different way.

I was very pleased to be asked to write a book on these challenges and opportunities. It was both an exhilarating and a daunting request. It was exhilarating in that it allowed me the opportunity to make a public contribution to an important debate, which will have profound implications on the future of my chosen profession. Moreover, our cumulative decisions on the adoption of new Internet-based training could have important social consequences. They could influence who will, and who will not, have access to opportunities for self-development in the new economy.

It was equally exciting when, following the relative success of the UK edition of the book, I was invited to prepare this updated version for AMACOM. The opportunity of bringing these arguments to a wider audience was most compelling. It was a daunting prospect, however, because the subject is moving so rapidly that any material requires permanent updating and addition. It is never the right time to publish. Each section calls for a health warning that the information was correct in October 2001 when the manuscript was completed.

Two factors have encouraged me to proceed and face the near certainty that a proportion of my suggestions or predictions will be overtaken by events—or simply proved to be wrong. First, there is an evident need for a book that offers practical assistance for all those managers who are contemplating the transition to a new delivery of training in their organization. Their jobs will differ: they could be human resources professionals (especially training managers), working in information technology or knowledge management, or have more general line responsibilities. Whatever their titles and responsibilities, a book exploring the issues is required now. It should be written by someone who is himself or herself grappling with the problems. Second, I am fortunate that my two employers over this period, Ernst & Young and the Chartered Institute of Personnel and Development, have fully supported my endeavors. Ernst & Young gave me generous permission to include much material from the workplace. Many of my original ideas have been drawn from or developed as a result of discussions with my colleagues in the firm.

Martyn Sloman

ACKNOWLEDGMENTS

I am grateful to all those who allowed me to draw on their work and on their ideas. Many of these contributors have been acknowledged at appropriate points in the text. Particular thanks should, however, be extended to Mark Van Buren, Pat Galagan, and Stacey Wagner of the ASTD and Elliott Masie of the MASIE Center.

My former colleagues at Ernst & Young were a great source of inspiration and encouragement at the outset of this project and throughout its subsequent development. In particular, my conversations with Des Woods yielded almost daily insights and ideas that have found their way into the text. Others who had an influence on this and the earlier editions include Jim L'Allier, Mike Laws, John Odell, Toby Hoskins, Iain Thomson, Steve Knight, Richard Comber, and Sara Willis. Karen Jacques offered a most perceptive critique of an earlier draft.

Jennifer Schramm, Mike Cannell, and Lorna Munro undertook some of the work on the case study organizations. I am grateful to them and to all the representatives from the companies cited who shared their experiences and insights so openly. Kim Andrews typed and organized the manuscript and showed immense patience in meeting tight deadlines. Thanks also to Anne Cordwent and Jacquie Flynn, my editors, for their encouragement and support.

Most of this text was written in Norfolk, where my wife, Anne, has tolerated sustained weekend and holiday work on the book. She has been totally understanding and sympathetic. My thanks to her for her support in all my life's efforts.

INTRODUCTION AND PROPOSITIONS

Two related developments are combining to demand a new approach to the effective delivery of training in organizations. Both are a consequence of the information-rich or connected economy. The first is a step change in the capability and potential of technology-based training. The second is a shifting business model: the way that organizations compete and society advances.

Together these developments will transform the way that everyone in human resources will do their jobs and the skills they require. In particular, they will call into question the role of training and its place in the organization. They will redefine the distinction between training and learning. They will eliminate the barriers among training, knowledge management, and performance management. They will shift responsibilities among the manager, trainer, and individual. They will, in time, blur the boundaries between internal and external providers of training and redefine the market for both training products and delivery. And they will demand a reorientation of the learning support required.

There is a huge opportunity here. The rules of the game have been changed and everyone concerned with effective training must adapt. So far, the agenda has been driven by those who created the technical opportunities. It is now essential that those who will manage their application and implementation understand what is happening and develop appropriate responses. The alternative is a failure of credibility for the profession and a lot of costly and embarrassing mistakes in the organization.

This book is intended to help those involved in decisions on the provision of training to acquire a clear understanding of the underlying issues. Once this has been achieved, a realistic agenda can be

> ### Focus Point 1: Central Questions for Those Involved in Training
>
> ◆ What do we need to know about the connected economy (and how do we find out)?
> ◆ What do we need to do (what is the most effective organizational response)?
> ◆ How will the connected economy affect me in my organization (how will it alter my role and responsibility for training)?
> ◆ How will it affect our world (what is the wider economic and social impact on training)?

created. Every organization faces different challenges, but some basic messages apply throughout.

The relevant questions posed by the emergence of the connected economy are set out in Focus Point 1. The answers to these questions are wide ranging, so this book is part primer and part polemic. It is partly an introduction to the issues and partly a controversial writing or an argument. It is hoped that together these two components will provide a framework that will lead to effective decision making and allocation of resources. To assist application, practical examples are offered where possible. To signpost the book's scope and arguments in advance, I have listed a series of twenty-one propositions. These propositions summarize the main conclusions that have been reached as a result of the research and analysis undertaken to produce this book. They provide a framework to guide the actions of those involved in directing, managing, or supporting the training function, irrespective of the role or title. The propositions summarize an argument or offer general advice. Taken together, they offer a useful summary of the contents.

Propositions

1 The Internet changes everything, including training.
2 The drivers of Internet activity and development are business and commercial: They will shape and foreshadow developments in training.

3   The connected economy gives rise to a blurring of activities and of boundaries.

4   There is a danger of becoming seduced by the functionality of the technology, rather than concentrating on its use.

5   Training will move from events to interventions.

6   The distinction between learning and training is of value and should be maintained.

7   There will be a convergence (or blurring) among knowledge management, performance management, and training. All are responses to gaining competitive advantage through people in the information age.

8   E-learning can give new meaning to the concept of the learning organization.

9   A new paradigm based on learner-centered interventions will emerge. This will draw on business, learning, and traditional training models.

10 Training managers should identify the appropriate wins in their organization rather than let the availability of technology determine their agenda.

11 Training professionals should investigate the new business models. They should review their value chains.

12 E-learning will be most effective for the acquisition of knowledge and least effective where interpersonal interaction is needed for learning.

13 E-learning will be most effective as part of a systematic approach involving classroom and experiential learning with appropriate support.

14 A new discipline of learner support will emerge and should be encouraged.

15 There will be a renewed interest in learner motivation, learning preferences and styles, and time and space to learn.

16 Three distinct functional specialisms for trainers will evolve: design, delivery, and learner support.

17 A useful distinction can be made between hard technology and soft technology. The expertise of many trainers is in soft technology and this offers them an attractive future.

18 Any part of the training supply chain that does not add value will disappear. Other parts could well become commodity products.

19   Time, not money, will become a scarce resource. Monitoring of use and evaluation of effectiveness will become critically important.

20   Social inclusion is emerging as a key political issue. Trainers have the power to influence the debate positively.

21   More honesty and less hype are required if the training profession is to grasp the new opportunity to maximum effect.

Chapter 1

The Connected Economy

"Foresight is always better afterwards."[1]

The statement "The Internet changes everything" is attributed to Larry Ellison, founder and head of the software giant Oracle. In a speech delivered in Geneva in 1996, he predicted that the day of the personal computer (PC) was over and that the Internet was the vehicle of the future. Many of his competitors treated this prognosis with derision. Oracle prospered.

Proposition 1

The Internet changes everything, including training.

Twenty-one propositions are introduced in the course of this book. Proposition 1 echoes Ellison's statement. Of course, the statement as it stands should not be taken as a literal truth. Some things, those that lie outside the economic and commercial arena, may not be altered. The point is that the Internet is bringing about a change that will affect all economic relationships. It will alter the context in which we all operate.

What, then, are the likely effects of the Internet on training? This question is of critical importance. The pursuit of an answer must begin with an understanding and definition of terms, in the areas of both technology and training. It will continue by looking at the effect that the Internet has had on the market economy.

The Connected Economy and the Internet

The emergence of the Internet has been considered as significant and far-reaching a change as the invention of the internal combustion engine and its application in motorized transport. The information age, it is claimed, could herald as dramatic a transformation as the machine age, which introduced electricity to homes and mechanization to industry.

At the heart of what is happening now is the connectivity of computers and the establishment of a network with protocols—a set of rules that governs the transmission of data. Enhanced computer power has assisted all forms of activity for almost half a century. Gordon Moore, founder of Intel Corporation, is credited with the articulation of Moore's Law: Simply, this states that every eighteen months computer-processing power doubles while cost holds constant. The connected economy is something beyond more powerful data processing and offers huge opportunities in all facets of shared activity.

As is widely recognized, the most important breakthrough came in the early 1990s. Tim Berners-Lee—working at CERN (the European laboratory for particle physics) and building on earlier developments in information technology—proposed an approach and standards that would allow access to data from any source. In this way the World Wide Web was "invented." Berners-Lee's book *Weaving the Web*[2] contains a full account of the impressive early years. From the mid-1990s, use of the Internet has spread to the point where it has become universally recognized as the dominant commercial and social force at the turn of the twenty-first century. Focus Point 2 gives an indication of the magnitude of its impact.

It is about much more than the arrival of a new platform for the delivery of training.

Today's training professionals are therefore operating at the beginning of a revolution. More important, it is about much more than the arrival of a new platform for the delivery of training. The context in which the trainer operates, internal and external relationships, and

Focus Point 2: The Impact of the Internet

The U.S. Department of Commerce has compiled information on the time that it has taken for a critical invention or breakthrough to reach 50 million users.[3] The comparative figures are:

Radio   38 years
PC   16 years
Television   13 years
Internet   4 years

The speed of penetration and commercial impact of the Internet to date have been both dramatic in volume and consistently underestimated. Forrester, which specializes in research for the Internet, produces annual estimates of Internet trade. The April 2000 forecasts were titled "Global eCommerce Approaches Hypergrowth." This suggested that world Internet trade would rise from $657 in 2000 to $6,789.8 billion in 2004.[4] By then, it will represent 13.3 percent of total U.S. sales and 8.6 percent of world sales.

the role itself can be expected to undergo profound changes. The rapid developments in computer power have given the trainer the potential of having new information technology (IT) tools to assist delivery over the desktop using PCs. This impact of enhanced technology is one phenomenon; connectivity and the Internet are something else again. To understand the opportunities created by this upheaval, it is helpful to start with an agreed terminology. Some key definitions are set out in Focus Points 3 and 4.

Different writers and different organizations use different terms. A number of these will be encountered as their ideas and approaches are considered. In general, throughout this book, *e-learning* is adopted as the preferred term. It is used as shorthand for e-learning/e-training as defined in Focus Point 4—the delivery of learning and training that takes advantage of connectivity. Where necessary or appropriate, the term *technology-based training* is used to describe applications that specifically do not take advantage of connectivity. These could, for example, include the use of CD-ROMs accessed through a

> ### *Focus Point 3: Key Definitions on Connectivity*[5]
>
> ◆ *Connected economy*—an economy in which networked computers affect the market for goods and services.
> ◆ *Connectivity*—the process by which computers are networked and can share information.
> ◆ *Extranet*—a collaborative network that uses Internet technology to link organizations with their suppliers, customers, or other organizations that share common goals or information.
> ◆ *Internet*—the global computer network of digital information linked by telecommunication systems and using common address procedures and protocols.
> ◆ *Intranet*—a company-based version of the Internet. Large organizations have set up their own intranets as an aid to internal communications and may include training material or other information as part of them.
> ◆ *World Wide Web* (often abbreviated as Web or www)—the network of documents accessed through the Internet using the protocols. In a sense, it is the publishing side of the Internet, giving access to text, graphics, and multimedia information that have been placed on "sites" or "pages."

stand-alone computer that is not networked or connected to other users.

One of the more important implications of operating in a connected economy is that arguments about the most effective or appropriate platform for training that uses technology cease. Training will be delivered through the Internet/intranet using Web protocols. It will be accessed through PCs and laptops, feasibly using mobile technology.

The arrival of the Internet is a disruptive technology for the training profession.

In 1997, Clayton Christensen of Harvard Business School introduced the term *disruptive technology*.[6] This is a technology that overturns a

Focus Point 4: E-Training and E-Learning[7]

♦ *Training*—the process of acquiring the knowledge and skills related to work requirements using formal, structured, or guided means, but excluding general supervision, job-specific innovations, and learning by experience.

♦ *Learning*—the physical and mental process involved in changing one's normal behavioral patterns and habits. The value of differentiating between learning and training is discussed later in the book. As a first outline, however, this simple distinction should be noted. Learning lies within the domain of the individual; can result from a whole range of experiences; and can be positive, negative, or neutral from the organization's point of view. Training lies within the domain of the organization: It is an intervention designed to produce behaviors from individuals that have positive organizational results.

Learning lies within the domain of the individual; training lies within the domain of the organization.

♦ *E-Learning/E-Training*—the delivery of learning or training using electronically based approaches, mainly through the Internet, intranet, extranet, or Web (the e is short for *electronic,* originally popularized for e-mail, the transmission of messages digitally through a communication network). The terms *m-learning/ m-training* are emerging, with the m denoting *mobile* for wireless technology using mobile telephones.

traditional business model and makes it much harder for the established company, with its own cultural inertia, to embrace. Those who have invested time, money, and effort in the previous business model resist. The biggest impact of a disruptive technology may come when it gives rise to entirely new products.

The arrival of the Internet is a disruptive technology for the training profession. Christensen's analysis should be heeded. Existing models will be overturned; many trainers will resist. The losers in the profession will be those who, through cultural inertia, remain inside their own comfort zone and think in terms of traditional models. A starting point should be to look outside and see what can be learned from an analysis of the impact of the Internet on business and economic activity.

New Rules for Competition

Disruptive technology offers great opportunities as well as threats. However, to echo Christensen's argument, if the training profession is to capitalize on these opportunities, it must look outside its own sphere of activity. It must seek to understand the way in which the rules of economic activity are transformed.

As a starting point, it should be recognized that the Internet:

♦ Provides a new information system
♦ Introduces a new marketplace
♦ Offers a new system of communication
♦ Establishes new methods of distribution

Significantly, these attributes apply across all sectors of the economy. Historically, the initial impact of the emergence of railways was on the transportation of goods, although there was an unexpected subsequent effect on the leisure industry. The Internet has been pervasive from the start. It is global: It provides a worldwide method of sharing up-to-date information instantaneously. And it is cheap; it would be difficult to cite an innovation for which the costs of access were so small, which helps to explain the rapid spread of the Internet.

Much of the economic analysis and discussion has concentrated on what can be called the market effect: the way in which the Internet brings about greater competition through facilitating the exchange of goods and services. The market effect is summarized in Focus Point 5.

A practical illustration of the ways in which market forces affect recruitment is provided in Focus Point 6. It describes a situation that

Focus Point 5: The Market Effect

The Internet alters the nature of competition: It alters the rules of the game. This outcome is achieved through:

♦ Gains for the consumer through increased awareness
♦ Transparency of information—especially price information

This means that more markets have and will become commodity markets, in which competition is based on price alone, rather than on the superior knowledge that suppliers can offer the customer.

A market moves to a commodity market when the superior knowledge of suppliers becomes open to all. A good example is the travel industry. Anyone who wishes to book a low-cost holiday or a cheap flight can proceed by surfing the Internet and supplying credit card information on the Internet or by phone. As a result, the expertise of the specialist travel agent is devalued. Information is there for all to see and all can take advantage. Competition on price becomes more important and, therefore, the structure of the industry will change.

Transparency of information makes whole processes more efficient. It drives down prices and/or brings enhanced value to the customer by delivering other benefits. The new technology in general and the Internet in particular have unquestionably been a major engine in the high growth/low inflation evident at the beginning of the twenty-first century.

is evolving and in which the current impact of the Internet is less certain. It helps to introduce Proposition 2.

Proposition 2

The drivers of Internet activity and development are business and commercial: They will shape and foreshadow developments in training.

Focus Point 6: Illustrating the Market Effect

Online Recruitment

In February 2000, Forrester, the research organization specializing in the Internet, produced a report on online recruitment.[8] The report suggested that both recruiters and consumers agreed that online recruiting is more efficient than newspapers or hiring agencies. Moreover, online job seeking grew with Internet experience: "Experienced users were twice as likely to have searched for a job online than a new user."

However, the Internet was still far less influential than personal referrals or newspapers, and the uneven quality of jobs, unproductive résumé tools, and overdelivery of résumés are holding back progress. Most significantly, recruiters plan to increase online spending 52 percent by 2004, primarily at the expense of print advertising and search agency fees.

Given the inefficiencies in the current market and the possibilities created by the Internet, Forrester predicted the emergence of a new breed of site: "a career network." This would develop a longer-lasting, more valuable relationship with users and companies. Forrester defined the career network as a "one-stop career management site that aggregates multiple career services for consumers and recruiters and serves both in an ongoing relationship." Three components will reside at the heart of the career network:

♦ A *profile database*. By offering a range of services in career-related and non-career-related areas, these large sites will grow a profile database consisting of (1) explicit user data—résumés, salary levels, and news preferences—and (2) implicit data—interests and hobbies gleaned from online behavior.

♦ A *jobs database*. Aggregating jobs from numerous sources, this database stores detailed data on companies, job demand, and the types of positions filled online.

♦ A *matching engine*. This database engine not only matches candidates to jobs, but also learns preferences. Users who reject job matches are not shown similar jobs. Recruiters who reject candidates are not shown similar candidates.

The market effect is one way in which the Internet will affect training in organizations. Effective training is needed if an organization is to compete (in the private sector) or achieve its objectives (in the public/ voluntary sector) through the enhanced capability of its people. The skills required of those people will be altered by the new competitive environment. Moreover, the training market is a market like any other. The way in which this service will be supplied, and the roles and relative power of the agents or participants in the training market, will undergo a dramatic shift.

The implication behind Proposition 2 is that, by examining the way the Internet has affected business and commercial interactions, some important pointers can be gained for training. Again, to emphasize a recurrent theme throughout this book, those responsible for training can no longer focus on their own narrow environment. They must look outside.

The remainder of this chapter presents some analyses of the business effects of connectivity and the Internet. Each offers different insights, and where published works are cited, the reader is advised to seek out the original and, above all, reflect on the applicability of these insights to his or her situation. These are not asides.

The *Economist* Survey

On February 26, 2000, *Economist* magazine produced a special supplement on e-commerce.[9] The starting point of the *Economist*'s analysis is that the main impact of the Internet to date has been on business-to-business (B2B): transactions that take place between companies rather than between companies and consumers. According to Forrester Research, in 1999, 80 percent of e-commerce transactions were B2B. The main focus of the *Economist*'s survey was on retailing. Although the absolute level of consumer e-commerce was small, it was much higher in some sectors, such as retail, stockbroking, and publishing.

In all markets, the Internet has the ability to generate different price and exchange mechanisms. It allows product and price comparisons to be made using up-to-date information generated anywhere. It encourages auctions and other forms of exchanges to take place. Finally, it can bring together (and create communities among) buyers and sellers throughout the world.

The influence of the Internet extends beyond the trade itself. The Internet is used as a place to seek information. Critically, it allows continuous updating and real-time information.

An inevitable effect of this must be an intensification of competition. This will produce benefits to consumers in the form of lower prices and more choice at the expense of producers and intermediaries (for example, wholesalers), which, in turn, will lead to large-scale restructuring of industries. The rules of the game are changed.

The Internet does not replicate the social function of shopping.

Access to information on a global basis offers a huge advantage to the customer. Updating of demand is continuous, so companies can compete without investing in large physical sites or carrying stocks in warehouses. The offer to customers need not be a physical one. However, the Internet does not replicate the social function of shopping (the casual interchange with an assistant or fellow shoppers). Nor does it produce the change in atmosphere that some people enjoy in a shopping center. The *Economist* survey therefore distinguishes between "high-touch" and "low-touch" goods and services. The former are goods and services that consumers prefer to see and touch before purchase (shoes are a good example), and the latter are those for which consumers do not need such reassurance (books and CDs). To date, low-touch items sell best on the Internet. For similar reasons, the Internet may work well for replacement buys rather than new purchases. Fulfillment (the completion of an order and its delivery to the customer) will always be an issue.

Looking forward, technological change will improve speed and capacity—and availability of access. It is not a matter of snappier Web sites. The exciting opportunities will arise from the proliferation of broadband (or high-bandwidth) Internet connections to the home.

(Bandwidth is the capacity of a data connection or network for digital transmission; it is analogous to the number of lanes on a road.)

Another feature of e-commerce is that the Internet generates data, which can then be exploited. According to the *Economist:*

> Everything can be recorded: not just every transaction, but which Web pages a customer visits, how long he spends there and what banner he clicks on. This can produce a formidable array of data that makes possible both one-to-one marketing—directing sales pitches at particular individuals—and "mass customization"—changing product specifications, for instance in jeans or computers, to match individual orders to individual customer preferences.[10]

The Internet will also have a significant effect on the value or supply chain. This can be defined as "a system whose constituent parts include material suppliers, production facilities, distribution services, and customers linked via the forward flow of materials and the forward and backward flow of information." One argument, certainly in retailing, is that it is possible to eliminate many of the links in the chain altogether. Manufacturers can sell directly to consumers. Dell Computers is a good example: It has developed a successful business directly, first by telephone and subsequently via the Internet. The word *disintermediation* (the elimination of unnecessary intermediaries through direct transactions) has been used to describe changing markets for financial investment products for more than two decades. It is now applied to e-commerce. However, what may be happening is a subtler change: The Internet is changing the role and function of intermediaries, not necessarily eliminating them. This is a concept of considerable importance to the training market and is discussed later in that context.

The *Economist* survey specifically focused on retailing. However, the important thing is for those involved in training to seek insights, use analogies, and recognize opportunities from the changing business models. For example, if learners are regarded as consumers, how can the data that they produce when using Web-based training be used to customize and thus improve the product? As a second example, how will changes in the role of intermediaries (including their possible elimination) reshape the training industry? These, and similar issues, are discussed in later chapters of the book.

Blur

The term *connected economy* formed part of the title of an influential book, *Blur: The Speed of Change in the Connected Economy,* published in 1998 by Stan Davis, a senior fellow, and Christopher Meyer, director, of the Cap Gemini Ernst & Young Center for Business Innovation in Boston.[11]

Davis and Meyer argued that the economy (the way people use resources to fulfill their needs) is undergoing a fundamental shift driven by three forces:

♦ *Speed*—Every aspect of business and the connected organization operates and changes in real time.

♦ *Connectivity*—Everything is becoming electronically connected to everything else: products, people, companies, countries, everything.

♦ *Intangibles*—Every offer has both a tangible and an intangible economic value. The intangible is growing faster.[12]

Speed concerns the shortening of product life cycles and the use of electronic networks to transfer messages and information. Connectivity is about the use of computing power, not for data processing but for connecting people to people, machine to machine, product to service, network to network, organization to organization, and all combinations thereof. Intangibles is a more difficult concept to grasp. Davis and Meyer argue that the intangible portion of the economy has grown and that this growth has altered how we see the world. Services have come to dominate the economy. Information is more available and will continue to increase in importance. All products now have a service component; emotions, the trust and loyalty that people feel for a brand, are significant influences on economic activity.

Together speed, connectivity, and intangibles coalesce and interact to create what Davis and Meyer call the blur economy. A business (or other activity) is never at rest or in focus—everything is blurred. There is a blur of desires, in which product and services meld into one to become an offer and buyers and sellers merge. There is a blur of fulfillment, in which strategies and organizations merge. There is a blur of resources, in which people can no longer separate their working and consuming selves.

One of the continuing themes of this book is that those involved in training urgently need to consider the implications of operating in a blur economy. The word *blur* appears frequently in later sections of the text, with thanks to Davis and Meyer.

Blur is a powerful and seductive insight. Proposition 3 summarizes its importance to this book.

Proposition 3

The connected economy gives rise to a blurring of activities and of boundaries.

The concept of blur is apparent when some of the more popular Web sites are examined. In some cases, the underlying business model (the way that it will generate income and profits) is far from evident. The collapse in dot-com shares in 2001 could be seen as a powerful demonstration of the underlying fragility.

Sometimes, however, a site proves so popular that it almost achieves a life of its own. It can grow and develop in response to the demand of users, while still maintaining its original purpose and objective. Such a site is BBC Online. A case study of this site is the first of a series of case studies included at the end of the chapters of this book.

One of the current pieces of accepted wisdom in e-learning is the need to market sites. In the words of W. P. Kinsella's novel *Shoeless Joe,* "If you build it, he will come."[13] This is thought most definitely *not* to be the case in e-learning. In fact, as the BBC Online case study illustrates, sometimes if you build it people *will* come.

E-Transformation

This chapter has considered the changes brought about through connectivity, and how they affect commercial and economic activity. Connectivity is a key driver of globalization. Other forces that affect organizations are growing consumer awareness and liberalization/deregulation—relaxation of the rules that restrict trading. All of these forces reinforce each other and lead to a changing business model.

Connectivity is especially powerful. Boundaries separating different organizations and activities have become increasingly irrelevant (or blurred). Connectivity focuses on the exploitation of current and emerging technologies to transform business connections with customers, suppliers, partners, and internal stakeholders. The first three of these are currently served by the Internet/extranet, the last by the intranet. Next-generation technology will, of course, create new channels and blur these opportunities.

"E" is much bigger than just trading electronically.

It should now be recognized that "e" is much bigger than just trading electronically using the Internet. It is changing the way that organizations communicate and undertake transactions. Entirely new companies based on new business models are emerging. Focus Point 7 is drawn from an internal Ernst & Young document and summarizes the components of these new models.

Focus Point 7: Key Components of New Business Models

- Low-cost access to global markets/suppliers
- Reduced marketing and sales costs for businesses
- Twenty-four-hour shopping and reduced costs for customers
- Elimination of traditional intermediaries and emerging new intermediaries
- Further/cheaper connections between businesses, leading to reduced costs and increased agility in the supply chain
- Enhanced communication with internal stakeholders, leading to faster responses and improved speed to market
- New entrants into markets supplying completely new offerings, potentially eliminating existing players in that market

(Reproduced with permission of Ernst & Young.)

Ernst & Young has developed a series of tools to enable organizations to build an e-business model (*e-business* rather than *e-commerce* is Ernst & Young's preferred term). One of these tools, the Transformation Framework, can be introduced at this stage (see Figure 1-1). Such tools are known as single frames: a diagram on one page that captures key concepts in graphic form. A number of single frames are presented throughout the book.

The Transformation Framework is used to determine the extent to which clients wish to transform their organization toward an e-business and to identify specific initiatives to support this goal. More importantly, it explains the four stages of this transformation.

◆ *Stage I: E-Information—Dissemination of Information.* At this stage, the organization will have an online presence (necessarily seven days a week, twenty-four hours a day) that will provide one-way information over the Internet. Dissemination of information to whatever source (customer, suppliers, employees) is faster, cheaper, and more reliable.

◆ *Stage II: E-Commerce—Electronic Transactions.* Here the Web output is fully integrated with the existing processes and systems that serve the traditional channels. Data usage improves because data entry is required only once and knowledge can be disseminated and leveraged throughout the organization. Data sharing with suppliers is made possible.

◆ *Stage III: E-Company—Pervasive, All-Embracing, Embedded.* In this third stage, as much as possible, all functions of the business are conducted in a networked environment. E-business is the normal method for transactions among trading partners. Customers are dealt with online and the data are used to create greater loyalty. There is much greater efficiency in the supply or value chain. Greater awareness is gained through higher-quality information. This allows senior management to assess business profitability more rapidly and to manage processes more effectively.

◆ *Stage IV: E-Conomy—Reframing Markets and Industries.* This is the most fully realized state of e-business. Change extends beyond the boundary of the organization. A new economic system has emerged in which business is conducted electronically and each economic element is adapted to support e-business. An aggregated solution, or one-stop shop, has emerged. Everything from products and services to internal knowledge systems and learning is accessed through compatible electronic gateways. New efficiencies are secured as a matter of course.

The Transformation Framework (see Figure 1-1) is of particular assistance in emphasizing the stages of transition. It is a concept that can be applied across all goods and services. The left-hand column (marketplace, customer connections, supply chain, employee, fundamental) indicates the all-embracing nature of the change. The framework is reintroduced in Chapter 4, where it is used to assist in developing an agenda for the training professional in his or her organization.

The Effect on Training

It is now appropriate to move from a general consideration of the connected economy and its business impact to focus on training. The next two chapters look at the changes in the training environment, first by undertaking a brief overview of current developments, and then by reviewing the prevailing conceptual models and their relevance in the new connected economy.

It is hoped that the discussion so far has appeared neither irrelevant nor depressing. The changes driven by connectivity are profound and, to return to the opening statement of this chapter, the Internet changes everything. Much of the analysis, insights, and arguments that I have introduced in the wider economic context in this chapter reappear in different forms and at different stages throughout the book. I then attempt to relate them specifically to training issues and later to the role of trainers. My hope is that the discussion so far will have already led the reader to translate the general observations on connectivity to his or her specific challenges.

The speed of change is frightening but should not lead to despair. In the Old Testament book of Daniel, writing appeared on the wall during King Belshazzar's feast. The message indicated that the days of the Kingdom were numbered and that the king had been weighed in the balance and found wanting. There is writing on the wall for the

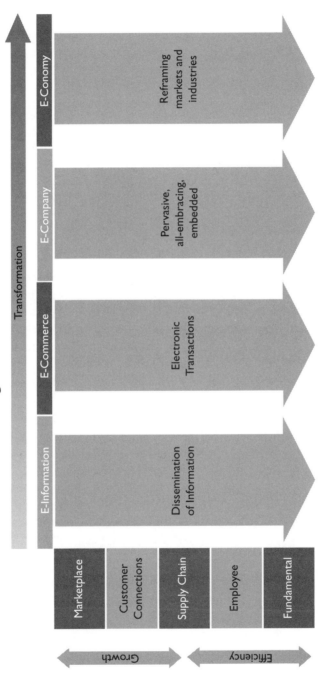

FIGURE 1-1

Ernst & Young Transformation Framework.

(Reproduced with permission of Ernst & Young.)

training professional (and, indeed, in this blurred connected economy there are all sorts of messages everywhere). It does not, however, present such a dire message. Instead, it demands that our practices and approaches be changed if we are to add value to the modern economy and our own organization. The start of that process is to understand some of the implications of the changes that are taking place.

Take comfort in the fact that our situation is not as acute as that of King Belshazzar.

A certain amount of uncertainty and anxiety is inevitable and desirable—no one knows where the changes are leading us. Time, however, is of the essence, and fellow training professionals can take comfort in the fact that our situation is not as acute as that of King Belshazzar; according to the Old Testament, he was slain after receiving the message of impending doom.

Notes

1   The aphorisms at the beginning of each chapter are all attributed to one individual: the baseball hero Lawrence "Yogi" Berra, who played eighteen seasons for the New York Yankees between 1946 and 1963 and subsequently managed both New York teams. He was renowned for the pithy but seemingly confused sound bite. The samples reproduced here are all taken from the following Web site on "The Jurisprudence of Yogi Berra": *www.law.emory.edu/ELJ/volumes/spg97/yogi.html.*

2   T. Berners-Lee with M. Fischetti, *Weaving the Web* (London: Orion Business Books, 1999).

3   U.S. Department of Commerce 1998, "The Emerging Digital Economy," *www.ecommerce.gov/emerging.htm.*

4   Forrester Forecasts, "Global eCommerce Approaches Hypergrowth," Forrester Research, April 2000.

5   Most of the definitions have been adapted by the author, but the following text is recommended: *The IPD Guide on Training*

Technology (London: Institute of Personnel and Development, 1998). The following Web sites are recommended for definitions of more specialist technological terms: *www.webopedia.com* or *www.whatis.com.*

6   C. Christensen, *The Innovator's Dilemma* (Boston: Harvard Business School Press, 1997).

7   M. Sloman, *A Handbook for Training Strategy,* 2nd ed. (Aldershot, U.K.: Gower, 1999), xviii–xix.

8   C. Li, *The Careers Network* (Cambridge, Mass.: Forrester Research, 2000).

9   "Shopping Around the Web: A Survey of E-Commerce," London: Economist Publications, supplement to 26 February 2000 edition, *www.economist.com.*

10   Ibid., 12.

11   S. Davis and C. Meyer, *Blur: The Speed of Change in the Connected Economy* (Oxford: Ernst & Young/Center for Business Innovation/Capstone, 1998) (*www.blursite.com*).

12   Ibid., 5.

13   W. P. Kinsella, *Shoeless Joe* (New York: Houghton Mifflin, 1982).

BBC ONLINE

The British Broadcasting Corporation (BBC) was one of the first organizations to appreciate the potential of the Internet. The BBC is a public-service broadcaster that provides education and learning, which will continue to feature heavily in its content and services. Given its success, there has been some controversy about the commercial implications of its initiative. Some competitors have expressed anxiety, and some politicians opposition, arguing that this is not appropriate activity for the BBC. Partly as a response, the BBC maintains two major sites: *www.beeb.com,* which is managed by BBC Worldwide, emphasizes its global reach, contains advertising and merchandising, and is unashamedly commercial; and *www.bbc.co.uk,* which is operated as a public service. The

subject of this case study is *www.bbc.co.uk/education* (now called
www.bbc.co.uk/learning), a pioneering initiative in e-learning.

Development of the Site

The BBC site originated through the activities of program makers, particularly Jonathan Drori, now head of commissioning,
BBC Online, and George Auckland, now head of digital media at
BBC Education. In the late 1980s, internal discussion between
them and others led to a recognition of the Internet's potential.
No browsers were available at the time, so the initial interest
was in textual fact sheets.

In the mid-1990s, momentum developed as Web sites became
associated with TV and radio programs. Particularly prominent
were the TV series *This Multi-Media Business* and *The Net,* and the
radio series *The Big Byte,* all of which considered the rise of IT. It
was recognized that Web sites could extend beyond fact sheets,
and funding was secured to explore ways of interacting with the
audience.

In 1994, the BBC Networking Club was established by BBC Education. This was primarily an intervention to help people access
and use the emerging Internet. The Networking Club acted as an
early Internet service provider.

The BBC Web site grew as more programs required a supporting
Web site, and there was a risk of incoherent content. To cope
with the growth, considerable thought was given to effective navigation tools, and the site has received plaudits. In 2000, BBC
Education Online won the Judges Award for the Royal TV Society
for its educational impact. This is one of the highest accolades in
the industry.

Current Learning Content

One of the significant successes of the BBC site is its continuing
link with the public examination system. It offers education support for the learning process, often linked with broadcast programs.

In 1996, GCSE Bite Size was introduced. It supports the demands of school examinations with cross-media activity: publications, a television series, and a Web site. The popularity of this site has grown exponentially. Server capacity has required updating to cope with the increasing number of hits. Demand is seasonal, but at its peak the site received some 2.5 million visits per week.

More generally, for adults there is extensive educational content material on a range of subjects, including science, history, and health. Some of the material is linked to programs, and efforts are made to ensure that it has a shelf life beyond the program's. Some of the content is generic and not so closely aligned with broadcast activity.

A series of approaches has been developed to encourage learning action with the public. BBC Alert (*www.bbc.co.uk/alert*) provides customized information about the whole of the BBC: factual broadcast output, Web links, and related local events. Users can visit the Web site either to view Web pages that match their selections or to register for a weekly e-mail version to match their preferences. Elsewhere on the BBC site, users can create their own version of the BBC home page using the "my BBC" facility. There are also many BBC message boards and moderated discussion groups, some of which are clearly recreational (the *Eastenders* site is the most popular), but others have an important educational content (the teen site is a good example).

Perhaps the most important feature of the BBC site is the sheer volume of its use as a whole (*www.bbc.co.uk*), covering news, education, and general interest; it has the highest access of any content site in Europe.

Future Development
The early development of the BBC site reflects an idealism and a vision about the values and importance of public-service broadcasting. Broadcast TV and radio can stimulate interest in a variety of educational activities—they form one end of a chain. At the other end is the consumer/user/listener; he or she has the power to undertake activity and create or produce results. In between

are intermediaries who can engage, guide, and communicate. The BBC initiative started as a content provider; some of the challenge must lie in influencing the intermediary parts of the chain. Inevitably, being the high-profile public organization that it is, the BBC's activities will be subjected to scrutiny.

Among future intentions is one to make available a full set of materials for the national curriculum in digital form. This will demand rigorous and complete coverage of all content.

For adults, the emphasis will be on the concept of a learning journey. This will offer an appropriate environment for interaction in individual educational exploration. Auckland emphasizes the importance of "bite-size, on demand and just in time." In his view, a learning module of whatever form should be available in slots of about twelve minutes' duration. The environment for adults should be as seamless as possible. Technology should assist, not intrude.

Drori sees other challenges ahead. The technological methods of access will include desktop devices such as PCs, domestic TV and radio, and mobile devices. As broadband develops, they will all be able to access consistent if not identical information. This will assist learning opportunities but present an organizational challenge for the BBC. The digital divide—the division between those who have the skills and equipment to get ready access to the Internet and those who do not—could widen. Other challenges will follow from the global reach of the BBC Online's service: Thirty-five percent of its traffic comes from outside the United Kingdom, and its online news service has a high reputation. It would be optimistic to think that the BBC can continue to be a pioneer; it does, however, remain an exemplar of a Web-based intervention.

Author's Note: My thanks to Jonathan Drori and George Auckland for their assistance in the preparation of this case study.

Chapter 2

What Is Happening in Training?

"You observe a lot by watching."

The previous chapter ended with a melodramatic indication of the change that improved technology and connectivity will bring to training. It is hardly surprising that people involved in managing or delivering training feel ill at ease. We are at the stage where there is a recognition of the magnitude of the change but uncertainty about the appropriate initial response.

So far the changes brought about by the connected economy have affected economic and business activity. To use the accepted terminology, these have been business-to-business (B2B) or business-to-consumer (B2C) transactions. Business-to-employee (B2E) changes, of which an improved approach to training is an example, have lagged behind. The fact that there are high-profile claims of a revolution to come hardly adds to the training manager's peace of mind.

For example, according to John T. Chambers, CEO of Cisco Systems, "Education over the Internet is so big it's going to make e-mail look like a rounding error." In its December 1999 issue, *Entrepreneur* magazine included e-learning in its "most important hot list to date" of business ideas for 2000. (Somewhat depressingly for some of our profession, virtual human resources [HR]—the outsourcing of specialist skills—also appeared on the list.) It argued that classroom training is old school and that online training companies that offer Internet- and intranet-based training are destined to be the new high achievers.[1]

There is no need, however, for those responsible for training to stare at the new technology systems like a snake at a mongoose, recognizing that serious problems lie ahead but fearful to move. What is required is, first, a realistic assessment of the current position, and then the preparation of an appropriate agenda. It should be recognized that more general competitive and social forces are affecting the role of training in organizations (irrespective of technology). These forces are considered briefly in the next section. Subsequently, this chapter examines the changes in organizational training, concentrating mainly on the developments that are occurring as a direct result of the new technology. To what extent have new systems become embedded? What is best practice? Has it emerged yet?

People as a Source of Competitive Advantage

Training may be entering a new age with growing respect for the importance of the function.

Regardless of the disruption caused by connectivity, training in organizations is in a state of transition. For some optimistic commentators, this transition is all to the good: It may amount to a renaissance. Training may be entering a new age with growing respect for the importance of the function. At the heart of this optimistic perspective is the recognition that the new basis of competition creates an opportunity. This can be paraphrased as "people are a source of competitive advantage." Some other influences on the changing role of training (and the dilemmas they create) must also be recognized and their effects considered.

Few employees in modern corporations have not at some time or another been on the receiving end of an announcement that "people are our most important asset." Inevitable cynicism has followed from downsizing and "involuntary redundancy": If people are the most important asset, they can scarcely be regarded as a fixed asset.

Despite this cynicism, there is a powerful argument that economic forces have swung the balance in favor of the capable employee who can bring skills to the organization. These staff need to be encouraged, supported, and valued if they are to be retained by the organization. It is a matter for debate how this should be done: What are the most effective HR policies under these circumstances? Focus Point 8 summarizes one expression that has received particular prominence: the war for talent.

Important social questions may arise on the position of those people who do not have these valuable skills. How can we ensure that they are not excluded from the personal prosperity and self-esteem that results from good employment?

What is generally accepted, however, is that the new basis of competition has led to a new approach to competitive strategy. Globalization; the growing awareness of consumers; the deregulation/liberalization of trade; and, above all, the communication revolution described as connectivity have already been recognized as self-reinforcing drivers of change. The focus of business strategy has shifted away from narrow economics (being in the right market and operating with the appropriate cost structure) to a perspective based on maximizing the resources of the organization, particularly HR.

Two concepts are of key importance in understanding what is happening in training. The first is the emergence of resource-based strategy; this is outlined in Focus Point 9. The second is that of the knowledge worker. The emergence of and importance of the activity of knowledge management are considered further in Chapter 3. For now, a knowledge worker can be described as someone whose work is intellectual in context; the task of knowledge workers is to share ideas and information and to bring value to the client or customer. To achieve this objective, they must gain maximum advantage from information systems. Competition in the modern age, therefore, is not about metal bashing or seeking to be the lowest-cost producer; it is about harnessing the creative talents in the organization to bring value to existing and future clients.

Influences and Dilemmas

Resource-based strategy offers a useful expression of the new opportunity for competition through people. Many of these people should

Focus Point 8: The War for Talent

In 1998 the management consultancy McKinsey produced an article in its quarterly magazine that received considerable acclaim in the human resource profession.[2]

Following a comprehensive study of 77 corporations and more than 6,000 executives, McKinsey argued that the best talent will be harder to find and more difficult to keep.

There will be a "war for talent" since:

> Superior talent will be tomorrow's prime source of competitive advantage. Any company seeking to exploit it must instill a talent mindset throughout the organization, starting at the top. (p48)

Large companies face some considerable challenges:

> A more complex economy demands a sophisticated talent with global acumen, multicultural influences, technological literacy, entrepreneurial skills, and the ability to manage increasingly de-layered, disaggregated organizations. (p47)

Moreover, small and medium-sized companies are targeting the same people sought by large companies and job mobility is increasing.

To win the "war for talent", organizations must elevate talent management as a burning corporate priority:

> To attract and retain the people you need, you must create and perpetually refine an employee value proposition: senior management's answer to why a smart, energetic, ambitious individual would want to come and work with you rather than the team next door. That done, you must turn your attention to how you are going to recruit great talent and finally develop, develop, develop!

(Reproduced with permission from McKinsey.)

Focus Point 9: Resource-Based Strategy

In resource-based approaches to strategy, the emphasis is on using what a company can do, rather than on where a company is currently positioned in the marketplace. Organizational strengths are developed, stretched, extended, and leveraged for competitive advantage.

John Kay, former director of the Said Business School at Oxford University, has described the importance of resource-based strategy in the following terms.[3] Resource-based strategy:

> examines the dynamics of the successes and failures of firms by reference to their distinctive capabilities—the factors, often implicit and intangible, which differentiate them from their competitors in the same markets and which cannot be reproduced by these competitors even after the advantages they offer are recognized.[4]

Effective strategy must start from "what the company is distinctively good at, not from what it would like to be good at, and is adaptive and opportunistic in exploiting what is distinctive in these capabilities."[5]

The main elements of resource-based strategy are as follows:

◆ Firms are essentially collections of capabilities.
◆ The effectiveness of a firm depends on the match between these capabilities and the market it serves.
◆ The growth, and appropriate boundaries, of a firm are limited by its capabilities.
◆ Some of these capabilities can be purchased or created and are available to all firms.
◆ Others are irreproducible, or reproducible only with substantial difficulty, by other firms, and it is on these that competitive advantage depends.
◆ Such capabilities are generally irreproducible because they are a product of the history of the firm or by virtue of uncertainty (even within the firm itself) about their nature.[6]

Kay places great value on resource-based strategy and indeed argues that the resource-based theory "unifies most of what is substantial and significant in our existing knowledge of business behavior."[7]

properly be described as knowledge workers. In addition, there are several critical influences and dilemmas that shape the environment in which the training manager operates. The opportunities, critical influences, and dilemmas are summarized in Figure 2-1. These were developed in my previous work.[8]

Key knowledge workers are often well aware of their own value. They have shifted their focus from employment to employability. The attractiveness of a career with a single organization diminishes when it is recognized that most organizations have a shorter life span than the individual's span of posteducation activity to retirement. As was recognized in the war for talent (Focus Point 8), job mobility is increasing. One major effect on training in organizations is the need to offer development opportunities: expressed at Ernst & Young as "the place to grow." A consequence (or dilemma, as listed in Figure 2-1) is the need for the training manager to balance the requirements of the individual and organization when allocating the resources devoted to training.

Figure 2-1 identifies another influence—that technology permits new approaches to training; this forms the substance of this chapter. The two remaining dilemmas emphasize the widening ownership of training organizations. First, there must be a recognition that responsibility for training has become more diffuse. In particular, line managers have been encouraged to carry more responsibility for the training requirements of their staff. Second, it is more difficult to manage training on the basis of a central control mechanism. Once devolution of responsibility is encouraged, the monitoring of resources must become more difficult.

The Impact of Technology

Technology should be seen as a means, not as an end.

Competitive and social forces are therefore creating a new set of challenges for everyone who is concerned with effective training—regard-

FIGURE 2-1

Opportunities, influences, and dilemmas of resource-based strategy.

OPPORTUNITIES	CRITICAL INFLUENCES	DILEMMAS
The key source of competitive advantage is now embedded in the skills and capabilities of knowledge workers.	Accomplished and marketable individuals seek employability—appropriate opportunities to develop their own capability in both the long and short term.	The need to maintain an appropriate balance between the requirements of the organization and the demands of the individual.
The new global economy reinforced by the information/telecommunications revolution and by regulation has changed the nature of competition.	Technology permits new approaches to the delivery of training—particularly dispersed access across networks.	Responsibility for the formulation of training policy and the management of its implementation has become diffuse: • a coordinated approach is needed on developing advantage through people • line managers carry more responsibility for developing their staff.
Resource-based strategy shifts in competitive emphasis from an external response to market conditions to an internal response based on the development of internal capabilities.		Targeting and monitoring of resource is more critical and more difficult: • more people initiate training interventions • much may be uncoordinated/inrecorded.

(Taken from M. Sloman, *A Handbook for Training Strategy*, 2nd ed. (Aldershot, U.K.: Gower, 1999.)

less of the opportunities offered by enhanced technologies. One of the central themes of this book is that technology should be seen as a means, not as an end. Undoubtedly, it can offer those directly involved in managing or delivering training an opportunity to do their jobs more effectively. Taking the broader organizational perspective, a realistic awareness of the current state and application of the technology is a necessary precondition for an implementation strategy. The potential gains from the new technology are about much more than effective training delivery.

Just what is going on beyond the hype? An overview or mapping of the current state of e-learning is presented in the following three sections. First, the work of the American Society for Training and Development (ASTD) is introduced and its helpful review of e-learning is considered. Second, some of the contributions of the independent commentator Elliott Masie are outlined. Finally, a review of the current e-learning technology and learning systems is defined and analyzed.

The Work of the ASTD

The ASTD (*www.astd.org*) is a membership organization that provides a regular output of reports and is a most useful source of objective information on developments in e-learning. Each year the ASTD produces a State of the Industry Report. Given the reporting lag, it generally refers to statistical information on activities up to two years earlier. The 1999 report contained a feature by Laurie J. Bassi and Mark E. Van Buren on training trends.[9] It could be said to have been produced at the high tide of optimism on the potential of e-learning. The section on delivery methods considered practices in leading-edge companies. In part, these companies were selected based on their approach to training delivery.

For these organizations, instructor-led classroom training as a percentage of total training was declining and was predicted to continue to decline. Bassi and Van Buren's feature estimated that it could drop to 60 percent of total delivery. In 2000, to be considered leading edge, an organization would have to deliver more than a quarter of training using learning technologies (the term preferred in the feature):

> Several technologies in particular are leading the way. . . . By the year 2000, 80 percent expect to be using CD-ROMs; intranets (70 percent) and the Internet (58 percent) ranked second and third. In fact, both forms of Web-based training are projected to triple in use between 1997 and 2000.[10]

The feature came to a clear conclusion: "The leading learning technology by the year 2000 is expected to be the company intranet. The typical organization expects to use its intranet to deliver more than 22 percent of its sources by that time."[11]

One other particularly relevant observation was the following:

> The percentage of courses that leading-edge firms deliver via learning technologies were not any higher than in the typical organization.

> In fact for some technologies, such as CD-ROMs and the Internet, the leading-edge percentages are lower. In other words, to join the leading edge, your organization won't have to use the technologies you currently have for more courses. Rather you'll have a greater variety of learning technologies to deliver your training than you currently do.[12]

On this basis, the following were the main lessons to be drawn from the ASTD analysis:

♦ There will be a shift away from traditional instructor-led, classroom training, which will affect both the ways in which training is delivered and the way people learn.
♦ In the short term (perhaps three to five years), the company intranet will be the most important vehicle for delivery.
♦ In the short term, about a quarter of training will be delivered using learning technology.

As noted, the 1999 report was produced at an optimistic, bullish time for e-learning. The potential was apparent; the problems less so. Problems of implementation were highlighted in subsequent ASTD reports showing that there had been a leveling off in the use of learning technologies. According to a summary commentary on the 2000 report:

Last year's report showed that the average Benchmarking Service firm delivered 77.6 percent of its training in a classroom setting and 9.1 percent via learning technologies. In this year's survey, these figures changed very little, with the percentage of training delivered via classrooms up to 78.5 percent and technology-delivered training, actually dropping slightly to 8.5 percent.[13]

On balance, however, the ASTD felt that growth would continue, and its 2000 report suggested the following reasons for the plateau in growth:

This leveling off in the growth of learning technologies suggests that perhaps organizations are finding technology-based training difficult to do well. Challenges that companies may be facing include technological barriers, cultural resistance to a new way of learning, and the challenge of ensuring that technology-based training is cost-effective and produces results that truly enhance individual and firm performance.

Nevertheless, there is no doubt that organizations are making tremendous investments in learning technologies and that these investments will continue to grow.[14]

This plateau in the acceptance of e-learning was reinforced in the following year's report. The ASTD State of Industry Report 2001 contained several surprises.[15] There was a reporting lag and the figures related to 1999. The survey showed a decrease in employer-provided training—the first decrease since 1996. Training delivered using learning technology as a percentage of total time spent on training was 2 percent in 1998 and dropped to 1.8 percent in 1999.

More important, "Use of Learning Technology" showed no growth. The percentage of training delivered via technology in 1998 was 8.5 percent and 8.4 percent in 1999, both below the level of 9.1 percent recorded in 1997. The ASTD states that "this leveling off in the growth of technology as a training tool suggests that organizations are finding the obstacles to implementing technology-based training difficult to overcome. We find this to be especially true amongst small to medium-sized organizations."[16]

This finding is now too important to be ignored. The platform is available; successful implementation has become the crucial issue. In the 2001 ASTD report, Mark Van Buren identifies several potential obstacles. These include negative experiences that learners had had with previous e-learning and the situation in which e-learning is delivered. These factors are considered in another ASTD research survey outlined in Chapter 5. On balance, he is optimistic: "We found evidence that perhaps e-learning is not destined for the history pages but is only taking a breather."[17] Most of us who are following developments in e-learning would agree. There is too much at stake to allow the barriers to remain.

There are many first-rate minds at work—in the vendors of e-learning systems, in corporate training roles, and in research institutes—seeking solutions to the knotty problems. The problems are real, however, and if they are ignored, continued implementation issues will be encountered. To put it bluntly, we remain in the age of learning technology rather than technology for learning.

Before moving on from the work of the ASTD, one other significant contribution needs to be discussed. This concerns its review of potential development in learning technologies. A useful 1999 report entitled "Trendz" appeared as a supplement in the ASTD's regular magazine, $T+D$. Some extracts are set out in Focus Point 10 and serve to emphasize the rich environment that will emerge.

Focus Point 10 may indicate the shape of things to come. However, what can be delivered on the current platforms is more than enough to excite all those with responsibility for training. Current multimedia training (whether delivered through CD-ROM or the intranet) can incorporate three-dimensional graphics animation, a choice of decisions in scenarios, and routing options that allow the learner to navigate his or her own path through the module.

One phrase entering the vocabulary is *high touch*. This is the use of leading-edge technology to replicate the softer interaction that comes with a one-to-one exchange with the tutor. High touch reflects a hope that this can be achieved. However, it is tempting to be entranced with the vehicle and to forget the objective of more effective training and enhanced learning. This pitfall is summarized in Proposition 4.

Focus Point 10: A Glimpse of Future Trends

In November 1999 the American Society for Training and Development (ASTD) produced a special supplement to its magazine, T + D.[18] This supplement sought to identify trends that were most likely to change the way that trainers worked. In its own words, the ASTD sorted through "mountains of predictions, opinions and guesses about the future of learning and work." Some of the trends that could affect technology and training were suggested by Jay Cross, information architect of Internet Time Group (www. internettime.com). He stated that the following will emerge "in our not too distant training future":

- Personal software agents that crawl the Web to screen and feed information to personal portals
- Connected gadgets and gizmos that simplify (and complicate) our lives
- Plug-and-play training modularity
- Learning standards that create interchangeable, Lego-like objects that slash costs and development time
- Personal files and programs that run directly from the Internet

Elsewhere in the supplement, according to the ASTD:

A new breed of technology is heading the pack and aiming to quell criticism of online learning as a static, isolating experience. In fact, it encompasses several technologies that connect online learners and the instructor in a virtual classroom. Synchronous online learning is already available at a fraction of the cost of higher-end video-conferencing systems.

Adding synchronous voice capabilities is the first hurdle. Existing systems that rely on teleconferencing technology are being joined by new technology, voice-over Internet protocol (VOIP) that allows real-time voice transmission over the same data pipes that carry online learning.

The addition of synchronous voice capabilities to online learning is only a stepping stone to the real objective—IP (Internet protocol)-based audio/video. Technologies such as VOIP will lead to low-cost solutions.[19]

(Reproduced with permission from the American Society for Training and Development, with thanks to Pat Galagan, editor-in-chief, Training and Development.)

Author's note: Synchronous describes the situation when individuals are all interacting in the same, real time. See Focus Point 17 for a fuller definition.

Proposition 4

There is a danger of becoming seduced by the functionality of the technology, rather than concentrating on its use.

The Work of Elliott Masie

The sentiments outlined in Proposition 4 would doubtless command the support of Elliott Masie. Described as a technology and learning futurist, he has established the Masie Center to consider how organizations can absorb technology and create continuous learning and knowledge internally. The center (*www.masie.com*) produces an interactive newsletter (*Learning Decisions*) supported by regular online updates (*www.learningdecisions.com*).

Masie possesses several attributes that make his analysis worthy of the attention of training managers. First, he is not associated with any vendor or manufacturer of learning technology. He is "learning-system neutral." Second, he is not seduced by the technology: He focuses his attention firmly on the learner and technology is seen as the means to an end. He argues that the *e*, as in e-learning, should be an abbreviation for experience, not electronic. The learner should be the focus. E-learning is not about computers and not about computing. It should be about communications with the learner, seeking to increase knowledge and encouraging meaningful interchanges and transactions that achieve this objective.

E-learning is not about computers and not about computing.

Masie also argues that our current stage in e-learning carries high risk. Doubtless some experiments will fail. The new learning techniques, if exploited effectively, can offer huge advantages to the learner. For example, knowledge can be adapted and disseminated instantly; "time shifting" is possible—that is, people can learn at the time most suitable for them.

Masie's philosophy and approach is entirely compatible with the messages contained in this book. His newsletter contains frequent analyses of the key issues in the learning technology, seen from the prospect of those implementing systems in the organization. This frequently allows him to promote a useful terminology of learning technology. Illustrations are provided in Focus Point 11.

Masie positions himself firmly on the side of the learner and is sympathetic to the training manager's day-to-day problems. He is good at

Focus Point 11: Elliott Masie's Terminology

Learning portals are popping up in a wide variety of flavors, all focusing on building a single doorway or entrance to learning services (online and classroom); providing a learning architecture including training management technology; creating an access point to the training/learning department; and providing online communication and collaboration capabilities to learners.

It makes sense, on many levels. If we can create a simpler way for training professionals or learners to access critical resources, it is a win! If we can help learners make better learning choices, it is a win! If we can provide a simple way for organizations to access the capabilities of learning collaboration or training management systems through a portal site, it is a win!

(From *Learning Decisions*, February 2000.)

Digital Surround

The recipe for a Digital Surround is quite simple. Take a traditional instructor-led, classroom-based training experience and enhance the offering by adding technology before, during and after the in-person meeting. Digital Surrounds are the place where e-learning is spreading most quickly with organizations and where some of the biggest returns on investment can be accomplished quickly.

(From *Learning Decisions*, March 2000.)

articulating the benefits of learning technology, and the concept of a digital surround (see Focus Point 11) is particularly attractive. His concept of supporting training before, during, and after the in-person meeting, coupled with the shift away from the classroom and instructor-led training, introduces Proposition 5.

Proposition 5

Training will move from events to interventions.

Irrespective of the introduction of e-learning, the tendency has been for the delivery of training in more readily available chunks. Modularization (delivering information in smaller segments) has become a popular theme as classroom events have become shorter; e-learning can assist in this process and in making a prevalent trainer's sound bite a reality: We must shift from "just in case" training to "just in time."

E-Learning Systems

This section attempts to map a learning system. A learning system can be described as a multifaceted software package that provides an e-learning solution. There is a booming market in the development of such systems, fueled by venture capital companies anxious to reap the benefits of the new technological opportunities. A new industry of vendors of such systems has emerged. Their activities have dictated much of the professional agenda.

Undoubtedly, these vendors are making a positive contribution by increasing awareness of the potential gains from e-learning. There is nothing wrong with a supply-side initiative. Markets are not all demand led. If they were, we would still be using carbon paper rather than the undesired (at the time) invention called the photocopier. The problems with new, hitherto-unimagined products generated from technological breakthroughs is that you cannot imagine them until you have seen them.

Everyone who is concerned with effective training must, however, retain primary focus on the needs of the learner. Proposition 4 should be committed to memory. Keeping a watchful eye on developments in learning systems is part of that process.

Figure 2-2 is meant to assist in understanding the functions that can be delivered by a learning system. It is entitled "hard" technology to distinguish it from a similar mapping based on the softer aspects of implementation, which is introduced in Chapter 6. The headings used in Figure 2-2 should become clearer in the context of the case studies developed in Chapter 4. However, the following definitions may assist:

♦ *Context*—the style of the learning portal (see Focus Point 11). What sort of information does the individual receive on entry and to what extent is it customized for the organization and individual?

FIGURE 2-2
E-learning system architecture: hard technology.

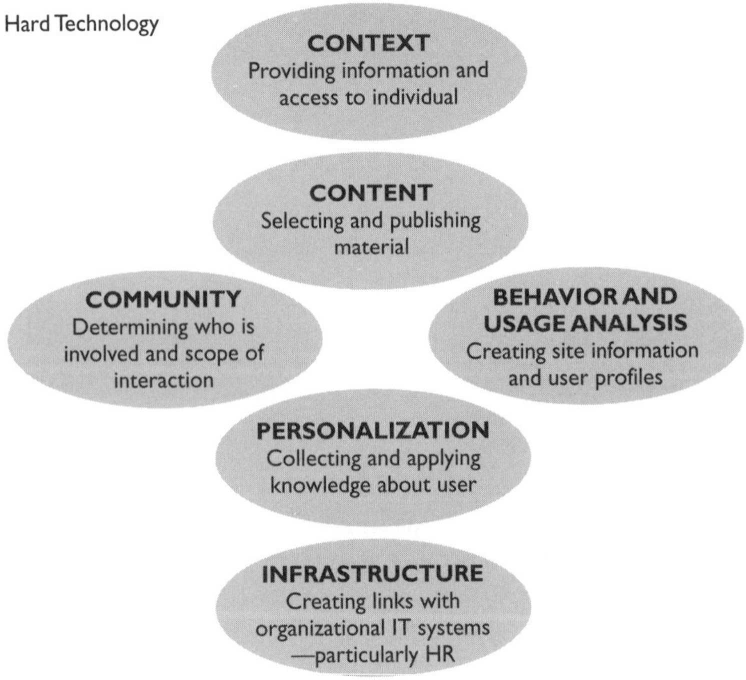

Hard Technology

CONTEXT
Providing information and access to individual

CONTENT
Selecting and publishing material

COMMUNITY
Determining who is involved and scope of interaction

BEHAVIOR AND USAGE ANALYSIS
Creating site information and user profiles

PERSONALIZATION
Collecting and applying knowledge about user

INFRASTRUCTURE
Creating links with organizational IT systems —particularly HR

♦ *Content*—the material that is made available to the learner through the system. Some systems are "content agnostic"; that is, they manage content generated elsewhere. Other systems are linked to particular suppliers of content or have made arrangements (often in the form of alliances) with providers of training materials (business schools or management consultancies).

♦ *Personalization*—Is the system capable of customization to the individual learner's own requirements? This extends beyond the design of the portal; it is about adapting the individual information and learning needs.

♦ *Community*—Who is involved in using the system? Is it purely internal staff? Is it global? Are outside organizers (suppliers, external consultants, and academics) given access rights and can they participate?

♦ *Behavior and usage analysis*—Has the system a recording process that allows the organization to collect the statistics needed to determine usage by predetermined organizational segments? Can individual use be monitored?

♦ *Infrastructure*—the link with other organizational IT systems. How does it relate to training records and recording and any billing or charging system? What is the link with performance management systems?

Some of these terms (personalization is an obvious example) will be features of the future development in learning systems rather than current packages. Nevertheless, as a review of the systems demonstrated at training conferences will indicate, all are available in some existing technology. Regardless of current purchasing intentions, developments in the market for e-learning must be of interest to the trainer. One current development, which is of particular interest to the smaller organization, is the application service provider (ASP) option. This offers an alternative approach for the provision of infrastructure and is described more fully in Focus Point 12.

There has been an enormous improvement in the ambition and sophistication of learning technology—and evidence of massive progress still to come. Almost anything that a thoughtful trainer could ask of technology to assist learning is there in embryonic form or is at the least the subject of sensible and purposeful discussion. Current

Focus Point 12: Application Service Providers

The delivery of e-learning content using ASPs has emerged as an attractive option for some organizations. The principle is straight-forward: Rather than installing the software or learning manage-ment systems on the organization's own system, an arrangement is made for it to be hosted elsewhere. A contract is made with a vendor for it to run the system on its facilities. Material is then accessed by the customer organization's staff through the Internet. The learning content and portal can be branded with the customer organization's logo.

Such arrangements have been a growing feature of the e-learning landscape since the late 1990s. The model harks back to the computer bureau of the 1970s; they are another manifestation of the broader business move to outsourced solutions.

There are evident advantages and disadvantages of this approach. It could offer a comparatively cheap and hassle-free option and be a quick way to introduce e-learning. However, there are practical issues to be resolved about firewalls and security; some IT departments are uncomfortable with what they regard as outsourcing by stealth. In addition, solutions that are developed and hosted in-house may permit a greater integration with other business systems as well as greater customization for the organization.

activity and improvements seem to be focused on two areas, and both are delivered at the individual learner's desktop. One focus is on reusable Web-based training modules, which can be purchased from any source or generated within the organization. The other is on synchronous real-time lessons delivered by subject matter experts using visual and audio links (and allowing the learner the opportunity to ask questions via audio or e-mail messaging). One of the plenary speakers at the 2001 ASTD Conference, Alison Rossett, referred to these two categories as "the stuff and the stir."

Development of the "stuff," the learning modules or objects, will be given a huge and helpful impetus by the progress in new industry standards for e-learning. The detail is unbelievably complex—the principle is straightforward. The intention is to set protocols so that technology in e-learning can work together no matter who built them. E-mail would not work without such standards.

In e-learning, standards will allow learning objects (a precise, if clumsy item defined as any entity, digital or nondigital, that may be used for learning education or training) to be developed by a company, educational institute, or individual trainer and accessed by users in another organization. Initially, the U.S. Government provided the first impetus for the development of e-learning standards; now it has gained momentum through the support of providers of e-learning systems.

The committees working on the development of SCORM (an ugly acronym for Shareable Content Object Reference Model) deserve all our thanks, though if successful the greatest tribute to their work will be that nobody will remember that it was necessary. We will take the movement of e-learning across systems for granted.

Given its commercial attractions, there has been a proliferation of organizations that have sought entry into the e-learning market. Generally, their product offering has reflected their business background. Software companies have concentrated on systems; publishing houses have concentrated on content. Many suppliers have sought directly or through alliances to offer the full range of functions indicated in Figure 2-2. Universities have sought to enter the market, and some corporate organizations have successfully developed systems and approaches in-house and then offered them on the open market. One example of the latter is the Intellinex approach developed within Ernst & Young, which forms the basis of the first of this chapter's case studies. It outlines the development and scope of the Intellinex system. Some of the issues and problems involved in implementing global e-learning are outlined in a case study in Chapter 5.

The latter three case studies give an indication of the pace and range of developments in e-learning systems. IBM's Global E-Learning model was awarded prize recognition at the 2001 ASTD conference as an excellent example of a tiered approach to delivering learning programs. The case study on the introduction of mentoring workshops at Hewlett-Packard using an approach known as the virtual classroom is an excellent example of the "stir." Both of these case studies are based on experience in large organizations. The final case study, on the Center for Performance Improvement, shows how it is now possible to take purposeful initiative on a much smaller scale.

Despite these compelling examples of good practice, generally our technology has not been developed for learning purposes. To date, training managers have been obliged to take advantage of developments (for example, the company intranet) that were introduced for wider organizational/commercial purposes. Now technological barriers are diminishing. Many of the hurdles to e-learning, such as lack of interactivity, content availability, technological standards, and bandwidth, are currently being addressed. Given these circumstances, two general points can be made. First, and this has been the main continuing theme of this chapter, the change will be profound and will extend beyond enhanced delivery. Second, there is a likelihood that a whole new approach to training and learning will be required as a consequence. What form this could take is considered in the next chapter.

Notes

1 *Entrepreneur,* December 1999 (*www.entrepreneur.com*).

2 E. G. Chambers, M. Foulon, H. Handfield-Jones, S. M. Hankin, and E. G. Michaels III, "The War for Talent," *McKinsey Quarterly* (1998): 44–57 (*www.mckinsey.com*).

3 J. Kay, *The Business of Economics* (Oxford: Oxford University Press, 1996).

4 Ibid., vi.

5 Ibid., 43.

6 Ibid., 33–34.

7 Ibid., 33.

8 M. Sloman, *A Handbook for Training Strategy,* 2nd ed. (Aldershot, U.K.: Gower, 1999).

9 L. J. Bassi and M. E. Van Buren, *Sharpening the Leading Edge: The ASTD State of Industry Report* (Alexandria, Va.: ASTD, 1999).

10   Ibid., 7.

11   Ibid.

12   Ibid.

13   D. P. McMurrer, M. E. Van Buren, and W. H. Woodwell Jr., *The ASTD 2000 State of Industry Report* (Alexandria, Va.: ASTD, 2000), 15.

14   Ibid., 15.

15   M. E. Van Buren, *The ASTD 2001 State of Industry Report* (Alexandria, Va.: ASTD, 2001).

16   Ibid., 4.

17   Ibid., 17.

18   D. Abernathy, H. Allerton, T. Barron, and J. Salopek, "Trendz," *Training and Development,* November 1999.

19   Ibid.

THE ERNST & YOUNG INTELLINEX INITIATIVE

Ernst & Young is a leading business advisory firm employing some 77,000 people worldwide. The Americas as a whole is the firm's largest base, employing 31,000 people, and the United Kingdom, with 8,200 employees, is second. There are significant practices in the major European countries as well as in Australia and the Pacific Rim. Clients are offered a wide range of business services with advisory/audit and tax, corporate advisory, and information systems predominating.

Intellinex is the e-learning venture of Ernst & Young. It was established within the firm in May 2000 to take advantage of emerging market opportunities. At that time, e-learning had been widely identified as one of the most important applications of connectivity. Ernst & Young was well placed because it had already committed considerable resources, over a period of years, to the development of an approach to e-learning and the associated technology and infrastructure. The resulting product, LEAP (Learning Environment to Accelerate Performance), has been subsequently promoted internally within the firm and made available to clients.

Over time Ernst & Young/Intellinex have created a comprehensive learning system with multiple components. Such systems, and any visit to a conference or exhibition will reveal no shortage of competitors, present a considerable challenge to traditional patterns of training organizations and delivery.

The early work on learning systems within Ernst & Young took place in the 1990s. This was a particularly successful period for business consulting. Resources were made available to the firm to fund a special project. An intriguing question arose: How would subject matter experts design training if they, rather than training professionals, had this responsibility? Clearly, rapid developments in IT had given rise to all sorts of new possibilities. This question is particularly compelling within Ernst & Young because much of the internal training relates to highly technical advisory and tax matters on which specialists have much of the expertise. Sharing that knowledge across the organization could generate considerable business advantages, but these specialists do not necessarily have skills in classroom training. Initial success led to rapid product development. This was accelerated when the e-learning system was shown to external clients in support of efforts addressing the knowledge transfer aspects of broader business initiatives.

From these beginnings, the use of e-learning within Ernst & Young has developed to the extent that a major global initiative is now taking place. This is considered as a separate case study in Chapter 5. Externally, Intellinex has a client list that includes organizations as diverse as Dow Chemical, Eli Lilly and Company, Glaxo Smith Kline, Cisco Systems, JP Morgan Chase, and GE Capital Services. Cisco Systems is a particularly interesting example because it is using Intellinex services and technology to manage the creation and delivery of learning to Cisco channel partners around the world.

Products and Systems

Intellinex emphasizes the comprehensive nature of its e-learning services (and a commitment to tailor them to its clients' needs).

Performance consulting support (Intellinex's preferred term) is seen as essential for effective implementation and to maximize benefits from the system. However, for the purposes of this case study, it is helpful to list the major components of Intellinex's product range and services:

♦ A learning management system (LMS) offers organizations the facility to deliver content to the learner using the corporate intranet or the Internet. It also offers tracking, recording, and reporting information on usage. Over time this will evolve into a personal development and competence management system. It will then be a component in an e-HR management approach.

♦ Two significant learning channels are available. These are, first, stand-alone Web-based modules accessed at the individual's PC and, second, a connected classroom described as a technology center featuring technology-based and instructor-led features. This allows synchronous learning in a virtual environment.

♦ A learning development system allows nonprogrammers (and nontrainers) to author content (to write and develop using specially designed tools and templates). Over time this has become part of a broader learning content management system. In this way the authoring tool is part of "cycle of content."

♦ Off-the-shelf content developed both by Intellinex and other suppliers is delivered in the form of short learning modules.

Other services concern the technology platform. There is a range of alternatives for hosting the LMS depending on the client's technology architecture.

Some Important Issues

Ernst & Young/Intellinex have, by industry standards, been involved in e-learning for a considerable time. They have had the advantage of a large internal population that has acted as a laboratory for product development. Of particular interest are how the focus of what they have to offer clients has developed and the issues that they now regard as important.

A first observation concerns what could be described as product mix. Two channels now predominate. Both are delivered at the individual learner's desktop: reusable Web-based training modules, and real-time lessons delivered by subject matter. These are the "stuff and stir" discussed earlier.

The distribution of learning through satellite broadcasts, which featured prominently as an alternative in the early stages, has proved prohibitively expensive. In addition, in common with the general acceptance of blended learning (see Chapter 4), Intellinex emphasizes that, however the technologies develop, learning in the classroom will always be a prominent part of the solution, especially in soft-skills training.

Where Intellinex can claim a particular advantage is in its early recognition of the importance of learning development or authoring systems. This is an area where considerable initiatives can be expected from suppliers. Indeed, Bob Blondin, Intellinex's chief learning strategist, believes that LMSs are becoming commodity products with increasing emphasis on cost and limited opportunities for differentiation or enhancement. Developing in-house material for the Web, through the use of authoring tools, is a challenging area with huge opportunities for improvement. Many of these challenges demand new approaches on instructional design. According to Blondin:

> Implicit in the current model is the assumption that there is an instructor in the classroom who will add value. He or she will adjust the material to the needs of the learner of the day. Web-based learning products must stand on their own content and design. Learner reaction—across a whole range of users—must be anticipated at the design stage. The authoring tool-kits and templates will need to be very sophisticated: They must remind and assist authors to produce material that can stand on its own.

Author's Note: My thanks to Bob Blondin and Des Woods for their assistance in the preparation of this case study.

IBM'S GLOBAL E-LEARNING MODEL

In 1997, IBM undertook a global benchmark study to determine its approach to the delivery of training using technological enablers. It found that two models were predominant at the time. The first involved the transfer of appropriate topics to computer-based training, then using mainly CD-ROMs. Typical topics (or subjects on the training curriculum) to be transferred would generally be chosen from the IT curriculum: JavaScript or HTML, for example. These were thought to be "suitable" for this approach. The second model was to take a whole course and shift its contents to the Web or CD-ROM. Such courses could involve both knowledge and skills elements. The courses selected would be either high-profile events or events that had a large course throughput.

Nancy Lewis, head of global management development, felt that neither model was appropriate for the learning needs of the 30,000 IBM staff worldwide. Instead, IBM decided to develop and deliver its own solution. It approached the problem from the perspective of curriculum design. What were the appropriate training methods or training media to be used for each learning objective?

The Model

After detailed exploration, IBM developed a four-tier model called (ahead of its time) the e-learning model. The tiers were in turn:

- Information and awareness
- Understanding and beginning of practice
- Collaborative learning
- Face-to-face intervention

Delivering learning through this model demands the consideration of the most effective approach at each stage and the deliberate and systematic orchestration of training throughout.

At the first introductory tier, information and awareness, the approach used is to put information on the Web. Summaries of best practice and just-in-time performance support tools are available in this form. Best thinking on more than forty leadership and people management topics of concern to managers are available, including materials from Harvard Business School Publishing.

These are supplemented with the regular publication of *Management Quickview*. Lewis emphasizes that no first-stage briefing should be longer than twelve pages.

The next tier, the understanding and beginning of practice, involves the use of immersive simulation tools delivered through the intranet. These are scenario-based, and different approaches are used depending on whether a person has a left brain or right brain preference. (The left brain is considered analytic in approach and those with this preference prefer a step-by-step sequential format. The right brain is more creative, complex, and fanciful.)

The third tier, collaborative learning, involves the creation of a virtual classroom, with peer group discussion using the Lotus Learning Space Groupware product. Here, managers learn teaming skills and create and build real-life networks while enhancing IBM's intellectual capital.

The fourth and highest tier, face-to-face intervention, brings learners into the classroom for face-to-face discussion. The other three tiers are used before and after the classroom to reinforce learning. Certain basic subjects may not involve learning input beyond the second tier. In Lewis's words, the tiered approach "begs you to think what you are doing at each level." More important, e-learning does not eliminate face-to-face education—it enhances it.

Applying the Model
Application of the model must be seen as a continuous process, with many learning activities extending over twelve months. Subject matter experts in any part of IBM can use the model to develop and distribute content. It allows the company to integrate and share training across the world. In May 2000, IBM formed a special business unit called IBM Mindspan to offer its solution externally.

In conclusion, IBM believes that the introduction of its global e-learning model has acted as a powerful signal of its commitment to its staff. It is seen as an investment in people and a tool for retention.

Further information on IBM's approach to embedding learning is provided in chapter 5, where time and space to learn is discussed.

Author's Note: My thanks to Nancy Lewis, head of global management development, IBM, for her assistance in the preparation of this case study.

HEWLETT-PACKARD MENTORING WORKSHOP

This case study describes how the availability of technology permitted a new approach to the delivery of a mentoring training program at Hewlett-Packard Company. Mentoring can be defined as the process in which experienced people go out of their way to help others reach important goals. To be an effective mentor in the corporate environment (and indeed elsewhere), a manager needs to acquire key mentor skills, including listening, building trust, encouraging, and providing feedback. This lies firmly within the domain of what can be described as soft skills, as opposed to the "harder" requirements for knowledge and information. A further consideration of mentoring and some of the issues involved in its delivery are set out in a separate case study in Chapter 7. This second case study involves a consideration of The Mentoring Group, a consultancy that worked with Hewlett-Packard in developing the approach outlined next.

The Virtual Classroom
The approach used in delivering the workshop can be described as a virtual classroom. The classroom proceeds along the following lines:

◆ Up to sixteen participants commit to participating in two two-hour sessions held on consecutive days. These participants can be in any location.

- ◆ The participants receive workshop materials in advance, which include a prestudy exercise.
- ◆ At the fixed time, the participants access the virtual classroom through a specified intranet site. All participants can view the PowerPoint presentation, which is delivered by a facilitator or trainer. A telephone link allows them to hear the commentary.
- ◆ Throughout the delivery, participants are able to ask questions and participate in discussion.
- ◆ Periodically, the participants are invited to share their thoughts in offline discussions using a telephone "bridge." This facility allows two or three participants to communicate with each other without involving the wider group of trainees.
- ◆ At intervals all participants are invited to break into small groups to practice the relevant skills aspect of the training. This is built around a role-play. After the breakout session, the facilitator debriefs the role-play with the whole group.

These points describe the main components of the workshop. Sophisticated technology is deployed to duplicate, to the greatest extent possible, the classroom experience. Other elements used in the mentoring workshops are the facility to deliver polling questions to gather participant reactions—offering them limited-choice answers to a question on the screen—and white boards to share information. "Electronic whiteboards" are used to capture a shared learning experience across geographical distance. At a certain point in the training, participants are invited to break out into pairs and asked to discuss mentoring experiences that had an impact on them. The participant responses are then captured, using a template, on the electronic whiteboard for all to see.

Overall, the session is designed to use technology to transmit material, provide access to the instruction, and allow feedback. Individual practice is also an indispensable element. The program can be regarded as a good example of what is, in the current fashion, being described as blended learning, an attempt to deploy different approaches and different delivery channels to maximum advantage. Blended learning is defined and outlined further in Chapter 4.

Implementation and Important Issues

Now that the technology and the module have been outlined, it is appropriate to consider the reasons that this approach was adopted. For some time, the ability of senior and middle managers to mentor has been critical to Hewlett-Packard's business and human resources strategy. Indeed, the mentoring workshop had been delivered in a classroom format since 1993. In 1999, a decision was made to transfer the program to a virtual classroom format and The Mentoring Group, which delivered the classroom workshop, and Hewlett-Packard began the process of redesign. Since then, some dozen or so workshops have been conducted using the new format.

Two main arguments were advanced for this decision. The first was the ability to reach more potential mentors: The workshop has been extended to include participants in Europe and Asia. The second concerns cost, particularly the elimination of travel costs. The classroom workshop costs at least $800 per participant (including travel expenses), whereas the virtual workshop costs only $180 per participant.

Undoubtedly, as the continued delivery of the workshop demonstrates, the approach works and has clear cost-benefit advantages. Important questions inevitably concern participant reaction. These are discussed further in the case study on CCC/ The Mentoring Group in Chapter 7. Specifically, Kathleen Barton, mentor program manager at Hewlett-Packard, makes the following observations:

> Some participants are pleasantly surprised. They find the technology friendly, and they like the interaction. This is evidenced by participant comments. "This was my first Web-based training. I thought it was great. The technology really works; the break out sessions were great," shares one HP manager. All participants love the convenience, since they don't have to travel!

Some participants who prefer a more active and involved learning experience may, however, feel a slight decrease in value. Barton feels that this is a function of personality type. Clearly, learning preferences is an important area for research consideration (see

Chapter 5 and the case studies in Chapter 7 for further discussion).

Finally, given the ambitious scope of this initiative, it is pertinent to ask, What problems have been encountered? Significantly, Barton's answers and examples center on ensuring that all delivery channels are in place and working effectively, "however much you prepare, check and double check." One amusing example concerned a trainee who tried to participate by using a cell phone from an airport, and by following a printed version of the workshop's slides. Her enthusiasm and commitment caused static problems on the bridge telephone lines and a move to more traditional telephony was needed for the session to proceed.

Author's Note: My thanks to Kathleen Barton and Hewlett-Packard for their assistance in the preparation of this case study.

CENTER FOR PERFORMANCE IMPROVEMENT, INEEL

The Center for Performance Improvement (CPI) is a department of the Idaho National Engineering and Environmental Laboratory's (INEEL) Training Directorate. Established in 1949, INEEL is a multiprogram research, development, and engineering laboratory supporting the U.S. Department of Energy (DOE). It provides specialized facility and technical management, applied research and development, systems analysis, proof-of-concept engineering, technical support, and related services for various offices of the DOE. INEEL employs about 6,000 people. About half of these are operations staff, and the rest are either research and development staff or technical and administrative support staff. Educational backgrounds range from high school/trade school through Ph.D.

INEEL consists of several in-town offices and research facilities located in Idaho Falls and an 890-square-mile reservation (about three-quarters the size of Rhode Island) located about 45 miles west of Idaho Falls. Richard Holman, CPI manager, describes the site as "a little city" consisting of nine major facility areas. Each facility area has its own training manager and learning center. The development of e-learning content applicable to sitewide operations, however, is centralized at CPI.

The E-Learning Initiative

INEEL began exploring the potential of e-learning in a variety of computer- Web- and video-based formats in the mid-1990s, looking for ways to improve return on investment for training dollars. Employees working at a government laboratory are required to take a significant number of courses to familiarize themselves and regularly review relevant health, safety, environmental, and security regulations. With a relatively large audience dispersed over so many square miles, e-learning (particularly Web based) has become more and more popular as well as efficient. Approximately 15 percent of all training is delivered via e-learning, and that figure is expected to rise to about 25 percent over the next decade. This exceeds most companies' current utilization of the Web for the delivery of training content according to a recent benchmarking study conducted at INEEL by the ASTD.

CPI is responsible for leading out and supporting all INEEL-wide e-learning efforts. CPI provides front-end needs analysis, performance consulting, development of electronic performance support systems, and exploration and evaluation of new learning technologies and methods. According to Holman, e-learning at INEEL comprises computer-based training (CBT) (CD-ROM, DVD, and hard drive or local area network based) and Web-based training (WBT). Commercially purchased CBT is available only in the learning centers while the in-house-developed WBT is available through the intranet to all employees with workstations (about 85 percent of INEEL's population). Those without workstations can get WBT at INEEL's learning centers. Pilot efforts to use a sophisticated teleconferencing system purchased several years ago did not result in as widescale use of that system for training purposes.

Progress in e-learning has been commensurate with progress in automated record keeping and skills management. All the course notifications and completions are automatically tracked by a sophisticated LMS that INEEL has created and maintains in-house. This system, TRAIN, short for the Training Resources and Information Network, has evolved into an LMS over the last three to four years and is now a central component of INEEL's seamless WBT delivery and evaluation process.

Choice of Technology

Early on, CPI did purchase CBT development tools (which have since been abandoned) and considered buying commercial off-the-shelf WBT course development tools and an LMS. After thorough investigation of numerous products, CPI concluded that building its own system using HTML, databases, and dynamic linking tools would afford it much greater long-term savings and flexibility. CPI, early on, decided to actively facilitate the intersection of instructional and information technology. The WBT courses themselves require extensive content customization not easily or cost-effectively managed with commercially available on-line curricula. To date, CPI and its customers are very pleased with these decisions. A singular Web-based development template and a variety of plug-in components have been developed to create more than 100 courses and learning activities. These range from simple required readings to interactive path simulations.

The central importance of a flexible system is apparent in the wide range of learning modules that CPI has developed. Most modules are quite short, requiring about a half an hour to complete, but some courses include eight to sixteen hours of learning, broken into numerous bite-sized modules.

TRAIN, the LMS, was also developed in-house. Brought in in 1995 from another DOE laboratory, it has been dramatically customized by INEEL. Whereas the original TRAIN was geared toward reports, the modified INEEL TRAIN LMS is process oriented—a dynamic application program interface.

Deciding to use in-house design meant that the instructional and technical capabilities of internal staff needed to be developed to the extent that they themselves could create, manage, and modify the e-learning system, including the LMS. Since 1998, CPI has developed more than 100 internal WBT courses and activities to be used on the desktop or at one of the INEEL learning centers. Robert Richards, technical lead for learning technologies and systems, explains how internal staff development moves CPI team members systematically from novice (rote) use of existing templates to more and more advanced skill levels where they can create whole new designs. CPI uses a "Web-based training and development checklist" to develop each course. The checklist comprises tasks for completion that need to be signed off before proceeding to the next step. It is divided into the following sections: analysis and design, development, training review, conduct pilot, and implementation. After the course is implemented, an ongoing evaluation is conducted.

Evaluation

CPI has also developed its own standardized evaluation system for the Web-based learning modules. Most WBT courses use a CPI-developed random exam generator to measure student learning. All of the WBT modules are evaluated via a Level One Kirkpatrick feedback system (see Chapter 7 for fuller details of the Kirkpatrick framework). This is linked to TRAIN and feeds into its database. In addition to the end-of-course evaluation, each page of instruction features a learner feedback tool. Learner comments and criticisms are forwarded to the learning module's instructional technologist and subject matter expert as well as CPI management. The student is then sent an e-mail acknowledgment explaining that the feedback has been logged and sent to the appropriate people. Pamela Barnes, technical lead for WBT development, views all of this feedback and uses it to learn which courses are doing well and which ones are not and why. CPI sees two main advantages to the evaluation process. First, it helps to improve courses by clarifying problems in the delivery, and, second, it gives learners a sense that they are participating in a collaborative project, helping to ease the "loneliness factor" that can sometimes occur in e-learning.

Problems and Challenges

Because TRAIN is intranet based, a current challenge concerns the delivery of learning off-site, particularly to learners in their homes. The completion and evaluation data on courses outside the INEEL firewall need to get back into TRAIN. INEEL has established several learning centers in nearby communities and has worked out a method of getting that data included in TRAIN. An Internet-based initiative is also being developed to address this problem, and Holman estimates that learners will soon be able to learn at home and automatically get credit in TRAIN.

Another challenge centers on the evaluation process. The Level One evaluation embedded within the e-learning modules is not mandatory. At this point about 30 to 40 percent of learners complete an evaluation. Whereas negative responses tend to pinpoint exactly what the encountered problems are, positive responses tend to be much more general. This makes it difficult to narrow down "what is working," when using feedback to help develop new e-learning modules. Further, it is crucial to address any computer literacy issues that may limit users in taking full advantage of the programs being offered.

The Future

The main challenge for CPI in the future is to remain up-to-date in its instructional and information delivery methods. This is critical in keeping its current internal and external clients happy and in ensuring that effective and efficient learning occurs. Another goal is to stimulate and challenge the instructional design team so that it remains enthusiastic. Because compliance-driven subject matter can be quite dry, instructional designers need to be exceptionally innovative and creative in seeking to engage the learner (maximize effectiveness) while minimizing costs.

Author's Note: My thanks to Richard Holman and Robert Richards for their assistance in the preparation of this case study.

Chapter 3

A New Paradigm for Training

"We made too many wrong mistakes."

The previous two chapters have set the context in which training will be delivered in the organization of the future. Chapter 1 considered how connectivity has altered the basis of competition, and Chapter 2 summarized the consequent developments in training. Before we consider how those who carry the responsibility for training can build their own practical agenda, one further stage in the argument must be presented. This is the view that the changes that have arisen from connectivity have been so far-reaching that they demand a completely new conceptual approach to training in organizations: the view that they demand a new paradigm.

Paradigms, Models, and Frameworks

A dictionary definition of a paradigm is: "a basic theory, a conceptual framework within which scientific theories are constructed." A change in a paradigm (popularly described as a paradigm shift) is important and exciting. It offers different ways of thinking that open up new practical possibilities. A historical example is when the realization grew that the world was round, not flat. This affected a whole range of perceptions, thoughts, and ideas from the abstract to the practical. When people disappeared without trace, they were no longer thought to have fallen off the end of the Earth.

A change or shift in a paradigm will have an impact on a whole range of constructs and ideas that apply across different situations and activities. It will necessitate the development of a different kind of framework or template to guide implementation in the organization.

Such frameworks will need to be redesigned in the context of the new paradigm. The frameworks available for training are considered in Chapter 4 (where the agenda for the organization is considered), in Chapter 6 (where the role of the trainer is outlined), and in Chapter 7 (where the impact on the industry is discussed).

Learning and Training

Two models have dominated our approach to training over the last two decades. At a crude level, one can be described as a training model, the other as a learning model. Much of the recent debate and discussion in the literature has emphasized the primacy of learning over training: The job of human resources development is to encourage learning. Training, by implication, is somewhat passé.

Despite the fact that it is no longer fashionable, training (as opposed to learning) is still a useful concept.

One of the arguments of this book is that despite the fact that it is no longer fashionable, training (as opposed to learning) is still a useful concept. This argument is expressed in Proposition 6.

Proposition 6

The distinction between learning and training is of value and should be maintained.

Initial definitions of terms were offered in Focus Point 4. A further discussion on learning is offered in Chapter 5, where the current body of information on the learning process is reviewed. The important distinction is simply restated. Learning lies in the domain of the individual: It is about the process of changing patterns and behavior. Training lies in the domain of the organization: It is an intervention designed to improve the knowledge and skills of employees.

The following illustrates the different domains. Some people who arrive in organizations learn rapidly where the limit and boundaries of acceptable behavior lie. They learn, for example, to claim the maximum expenses. So far, however, there is no evidence of training intervention to support such behavior. There are no courses available titled "Augmenting Your Expenses: An Introduction" or "Advanced Expense Augmentation." The organization does not intervene in this way; some people, however, learn (in this case bad habits) from others.

Traditionally, organizational interventions carrying the label "training" have tended to be directive—individuals have been told what to do and expected to do what they are told. Training course menus were published in the form of catalogs and individuals were expected to participate. Although times have changed, this still applies, for example, to professional training and training associated with qualifications.

Directive approaches are not without value in appropriate circumstances, such as health and safety. Generally, however, the modern economy has demanded more discretion, creativity, innovation, and acceptance of responsibility from employees. This has resulted in a shift to a focus on learning and the learner. The mechanisms that can be used are explored in Chapter 6. At this stage, it is sufficient to note that such mechanisms have included self-managed learning groups, the communication of learning systems or pathways, learning contracts, and support through coaching and mentoring.

Systematic Training

The concept of systematic training became increasingly accepted in the late 1960s. Essentially, it was thought appropriate to regard a training intervention as a series of sequential steps or stages. In most expressions of the systematic training model, these steps were identifying training needs, delivering training, and evaluating training outcomes. The benefit of this approach is that it focuses on the need to apply a systematic, disciplined approach to each stage in the process.

The model was firmly grounded in the scientific management of the 1960s and 1970s. A great deal of useful work was undertaken that built on the constructs of the model. Alternative techniques for needs identification and evaluation, for example, have been produced and promulgated. Various commentators have developed and extended the model, often by emphasizing the importance of introducing feedback loops among the different stages.

The value of applying such a disciplined approach is at its greatest when the problem definition (that is, the articulation of the training need) is clear and the population to be trained is clearly identifiable and large. A whole new discipline of instructional systems development (ISD) has been developed using a systematic approach. The emergence of a powerful new platform for training has given a whole new impetus for effective training design. There is, therefore, much to be gained from revisiting the underlying ISD principles. Figure 3-1 is taken from a 1998 ASTD report on the impact of learning technology on the activities undertaken by HR professionals. It expresses the ISD model in terms of learning technology.[1]

Although of undoubted operational value, systematic training has deficiencies as a model. The most important of these is that, at its simplest, it treats a problem in isolation. The cycle is not embedded in any organizational context. It is the responsibility of the training professional, once the first indication of the training need emerges, to apply his or her toolkit (the systematic training model) to come up with an efficient solution. It is essentially a reactive process, rather than a proactive one.

One competitive function of the training manager is to enable the organization to become more effective. In part, this must be achieved by proactively identifying and offering training interventions that improve the knowledge or skill base. This does not necessarily involve waiting until someone has identified a need. Taken in isolation, the systematic training model is unduly restrictive.

The Learning Organization

The learning organization may be better seen as an aspirational intention.

FIGURE 3-1

Steps in ISD and learning technology implementation process.

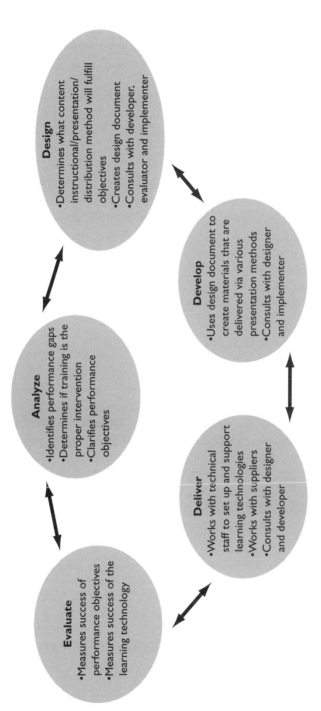

Design
- Determines what content instructional/presentation/distribution method will fulfill objectives
- Creates design document
- Consults with developer, evaluator and implementer

Develop
- Uses design document to create materials that are delivered via various presentation methods
- Consults with designer and implementer

Analyze
- Identifies performance gaps
- Determines if training is the proper intervention
- Clarifies performance objectives

Deliver
- Works with technical staff to set up and support learning technologies
- Works with suppliers
- Consults with designer and developer

Evaluate
- Measures success of performance objectives
- Measures success of the learning technology

(Reproduced with permission of the American Society for Training and Development.)

By contrast, the second important model, the learning organization, is wide in scope and ambition. It encourages proactivity. It is a learning rather than a training model. Unfortunately, the model is often uncertain in definition, and it is difficult to see what it means in practice. The learning organization may be better seen as an aspirational intention, rather than as a practical framework for implementation.

Much of the early impetus came from the organizational psychologist Chris Argyris, whose work has centered on developing individual potential within the company. In a book written jointly with Donald Schon, he developed the concept of single- and double-loop organizational learning.[2] The authors argued that organizational learning involves the detection of errors and their subsequent correction. If this detection and correction allows current policies and objectives to continue, the process is described as single-loop organizational learning. If, however, the detection and correction activities modify and change fundamental behavior, the organization can be said to have undergone double-loop learning; this necessarily involves learning from others, through discussion and a willingness to accept change. Organizations learn through the agency of individuals, and the appropriate climate must be encouraged to develop the synergy that can be gained through shared experience. Argyris and Schon's work is a contribution to our perception of learning: They wrote on organizational learning rather than the learning organization, but in so doing helped to develop the latter concept.

In 1990, Peter Senge's book *The Fifth Discipline: The Art and Practice of the Learning Organization* led to a huge interest in the concept of the learning organization.[3] It is a conceptually difficult book and one that is frequently misunderstood. For example, the fifth discipline of the title does not refer to organizational learning but to the need for a systems approach.

Senge differentiates learning organizations from traditional authoritarian "controlling organizations." The former are achieved by the mastery of certain disciplines, using the word in a broader sense; to Senge, a discipline is a body of practice based in some underlying theory of the world. He argues that five new "component technologies" or disciplines are gradually converging to innovate learning organizations. These are:

♦ *Personal mastery*—the capacity to clarify what is most important to the individual
♦ *Team learning*—based on a dialogue in which assumptions are suspended so that the team genuinely collaborates on ideas
♦ *Mental models*—the capacity to reflect on internal pictures of the world to see how they shape actions
♦ *Shared vision*—the ability to build a sense of commitment in a group based on what people would really like to create
♦ *Systems thinking*—the capacity for putting things together and seeking holistic solutions

Systems thinking is the fifth discipline because it is the one that integrates the others, fusing them into a coherent body of theory and practice. According to Senge, "It keeps them [the other disciplines] from being separate gimmicks or the latest organizational change fads."[4]

Senge's comments on team learning are of considerable value, but his central message is that such activity must not be seen in isolation: It must be underpinned by the fifth discipline. Ironically, someone who is revered as a guru of the learning organization should more properly be treated as a major critic of the concept as advocated, since it is frequently viewed in isolation from other corporate activities. In a sense, the organization's leadership must buy into the total concept before Senge's learning organization can be implemented. This makes an important theoretical construct but a demanding idea in practice.

Undoubtedly, the concept of the learning organization has excited many practitioners. The major criticism, as has been stated, is that it is too imprecise to offer a practical framework for day-to-day activity. As an illustration, consider the link between individual and organizational learning. It is easy to see that individuals learn—they accumulate knowledge and skills both by design (if they receive training) and by absorption. However, in what sense do organizations learn? Certainly the accumulated stock of learning held by individuals is of value to the organization; this has led to the concept of intellectual and human capital considered in Focus Point 13.

This is an attractive concept, but two questions need to be answered. First, what is organizational learning? Is it more than an addition or summation of individual learning? Second, if it can be identified, how can it be developed? It is easier to answer the second question than the first.

Focus Point 13: Intellectual and Human Capital

A simple definition of intellectual capital is:

> The sum of everything the people in the company know that gives a competitive advantage in the market.

This definition reflects the early writing of Tom Stewart, a distinguished writer for *Fortune* magazine. In 1997, he published a classic book on the subject.[5] Stewart pioneered the concept of managing intangible corporate assets. A company can be defined by its intellectual capital rather than its financial capital (machinery, property, and physical resources). Stewart presented an approach to discovering and defining a company's human knowledge capital, its information (or structured) capital, and consumer capital. In his book he defined intellectual capital as follows: "Intellectual material—knowledge, information, intellectual property, experience that can be put to use to create wealth."[6]

In 2000, Stan Davis and Christopher Meyer expressed the idea that a radical realignment of wealth is under way.[7] In *Future Wealth,* they argued that everything of value—including human capital, talent, and other intangibles—will be traded in efficient financial markets.[8] Human capital will become the scarcest resource in business. Competitive advantage will depend on attracting and keeping the best talent.

Davis and Meyer's challenging *Future Wealth* not only considers the implications (for the individual and the organization) of the development of efficient markets in human capital. It also considers the importance of new approaches to risk and advocates the need for a new form of social safety nets.

Without a doubt a climate or organizational culture can be nurtured in which individuals are encouraged to grow by sharing experiences. Where the concept of the learning organization has disappointed, however, is in demonstrating clearly how this can be done.

How can individual learning be stretched and leveraged for organizational advantage? One useful volume that explores this area is Campbell and Luchs's *Core Competency-Based Strategy,* but in general this has proved an elusive idea for the training profession.[9]

Fortunately, the emerging discipline of knowledge management can offer some valuable insights into organizational learning, which we discuss in the next section. The concept of the learning organization will be revisited later in this chapter.

Knowledge Management

The idea that knowledge can be actively managed to give a competitive advantage is an exciting one. It is another expression of a view that in the modern organization people are a primary source of competitive advantage. Knowledge management shares a conceptual grounding with intellectual and human capital (and to some extent the learning organization). It does, however, lend itself to more immediate practical application.

Much of the early stimulus and interest in knowledge management came from the work of Professor Ikujiro Nonaka, who, in 1991, wrote an influential article in *Harvard Business Review,* followed two years later by a well-received book he coauthored.[10, 11] Nonaka based his approach on an examination of companies that are "famous for their ability to respond quickly to customers, create new markets, rapidly develop new products and dominate emergent technologies. The secret of their success is their unique approach to managing the creation of key knowledge."[12] Thus, emphasis is placed on the creation of new knowledge; this is logically distinct from managing existing knowledge. To Nonaka, new knowledge always starts with the individual; the task is to make that personal knowledge available to others.

In 1999, the UK Institute of Personnel and Development commissioned Professor Harry Scarbrough of Leicester University Management Centre and Jacky Swan and John Preston of Warwick Business School to undertake a literature review of knowledge management.[13] The report sought to evaluate critically the available literature on both knowledge management and the learning organization from an HR perspective—to identify the key features of knowledge management and the learning organization and their implications for people management.

Investigating the link between the learning organization and knowledge management was important at the time. The idea of the learning organization had captured the imagination of many HR professionals. It did not, however, easily produce visible new activity beyond a general commitment to invest resources in developing people. It was therefore difficult to be certain of any impact, or, indeed, to find things to monitor and measure. Knowledge management, by contrast, did not originate within HR. Much of the stimulus had come from the wider availability of technology systems that permitted the exchange of information through shared databases. Literature on knowledge management was burgeoning, whereas literature on the learning organization seemed to decline. Moreover, the literature review conducted by Scarbrough and colleagues appeared to indicate that knowledge management was increasingly viewed as a product of the information systems/IT industry.

A cynical view could be that the IT specialist had stolen the HR professional's clothes. This view is unduly alarmist. What was and remains at issue is a need to provide a coherent approach to build organizational advantage. Scarbrough and colleagues mapped knowledge management and the learning organization in a wide context of managerial theories:

> As our literature review shows, interest in the terminology and ideals of these theories waxes and wanes. If we place them in their context, however, we are better able to understand what they say about the problems confronting firms; we can assess the importance of [knowledge management and the learning organization] separately from their ability to capture the attention of managers. The inescapable conclusion of such an exercise is that the terms [knowledge manage-

ment and the learning organization] will fade away and be replaced by another set of buzzwords and managerial nostrums. However, the demise of these managerial fads will itself be testimony to the phenomena which they seek to address, ie the growing knowledge-intensity of business, the impact of technology on relationships, and the importance of change and innovation. *These factors are not the product of fashion but of history, and in particular of a convergent set of forces which are unleashing fundamental patterns of change on advanced industrial economies.*[14] (Italics added)

A Convergence of Interventions

The last sentence of the preceding quotation is a useful introduction to Proposition 7. This proposition introduces the term *performance management,* which Michael Armstrong and Angela Baron defined in *Performance Management: The New Realities* as "a strategic and integrated approach to delivering sustained success to organizations by improving the performance of the people who work in them and by developing the capabilities of teams and individual contributors."[15]

Proposition 7

There will be a convergence (or blurring) among knowledge management, performance management, and training. All are responses to gaining competitive advantage through people in the information age.

The concept of performance management lies firmly in the HR domain (if we do not know something about improving the performance of people, what do we know?). Armstrong and Baron provide a good overview of the issues. Generally, performance management is about motivating individuals through feedback and targets; it is about providing development opportunities; it is about aligning performance to shared organizational objectives. New tools and mechanisms are emerging to assist that process. Most important, there is a growing interest in multisource feedback in which a range of views on individual performance is sought and fed into the review process.

A good illustration of this proposition can be drawn from some current experiences of Ernst & Young. Training professionals in Ernst & Young's U.K. practice are implementing e-learning technologies developed by the Ernst & Young Intellinex venture in the United States (see the case studies in Chapters 2 and 5). One of the key mechanisms is usage of virtual presentations in which real-time lessons are delivered to the individual's PC using visual and audio links. At Ernst & Young, this channel is regarded as one application on a continuum of virtual presentation products. According to Des Woods, the firm's U.K. head of learning and development, the training and learning professionals have found themselves as "owners of expertise" of an application that is of considerable interest to sales, marketing, and knowledge management. This will demand a new mind-set and blurs boundaries. His view is that this development is to be unreservedly welcomed: "It is no longer clear where the boundaries of learning end—and so long as it is effective learning, who cares?"

The aim should be to create synergies.

This convergence, or blurring, outlined in Proposition 7, arises for both conceptual and practical reasons. Conceptually, knowledge management, performance management, and training seek to maximize the contributions from people. All are interventions. The organization does something that seeks to improve group or individual performance by extending current capabilities, which involves proactive steps. This is why the term *training* rather than *learning* is used. As these activities are extended and aligned, it will become increasingly hard to delineate and put boundaries between them. Moreover, the aim should be to create synergies. Training interventions should not be seen in isolation. Wherever possible, the trainer should seek to identify and draw from models that encourage such a convergence of ideas. In this way, areas of overlap and efficiencies in practice will emerge.

Practically, it makes sense if the same technology platform is used. Apart from the argument for building on user familiarity, there are powerful arguments in terms of improved efficiency of process. It is possible, on the intranet, to move between a training module and a database that contains information in a repository. It would be desirable (and technologically feasible) to embed the latter in the former.

Put simply, from the user's point of view, all applications can be accessed on the same PC. Questionnaires, guidance, and advice arrive through the same route. If what is accessed is a Web-based module on, say, the new economic models that are arising from the Internet, it can be described as training. If what is accessed is a commentary or slide pack from the organization on how the new economic models are affecting the products offered to customers, it can be described as knowledge management. However, the distinction is immaterial. Similarly, if the user accesses a training module on interpersonal skills, it can be described as training intervention. If the user is given, through multisource feedback, an indication that he or she needs to improve his or her interpersonal skills, it can be described as performance management. If there is a direct link to an interpersonal skills training event (whether a course or a module available on the intranet), it becomes training intervention. Although the blur is not as evident as in the case of training and knowledge management, a blurring of boundaries has taken place.

There is an important pointer for the future emerging here. The argument can be extended to a higher level and runs as follows. Continued convergence, or blurring of boundaries, means that e-learning will cease to simply be "about learning." The techniques and approaches of e-learning will extend into key business process and become a change management tool. E-learning will then migrate beyond its traditional role as a form of training intervention.

To an extent, this is happening in practice already, albeit in the most sophisticated knowledge-intensive organization in the IT and telecommunications sectors. Here, information is delivered across the Internet/intranet to the PCs of customers and suppliers as well as to employers. This information could, for example, concern guidance on product use or details of business intention. To paraphrase Woods, so long as it is effective learning—who cares?

Encouraging the Convergence: Two Practical Views

Given modern economic pressures, a blurring among the different processes designed to gain competitive advantage through people is inevitable. Moreover, it should be encouraged. It will benefit both the organization and the individuals. As will be seen, it is at the heart of the new paradigm for training.

The role of the training manager is to assist the organization in achieving its objectives by developing the knowledge and skills of the employees. Connectivity means he or she must work in a different way. A blurring of knowledge management, performance management, and training is just one dimension of the new context in which he or she will operate. What is important is to construct a conceptual framework in which a strategy can be determined and practical action can be taken.

The remainder of this chapter outlines such a framework and presents the argument that it should be regarded as a paradigm shift. First, the work of two commentators, one on knowledge management and one on learning, is presented. I have chosen these two because they are most practical in their analysis.

Professor Nancy Dixon, based at George Washington University, offers a straightforward definition of knowledge in her book *Common Knowledge*.[16] She also presents an analysis of the use of knowledge in organizations. Her approach is of value in building a practical framework for knowledge management and in facilitating the convergence of knowledge management and learning.

Dixon uses the term *common knowledge* to describe the knowledge that employees learn from doing the organization's tasks. She uses this term to differentiate from book knowledge, regulations, databases, and customer information. Using her description, the acquisition and spread of common knowledge must be a form of learning. Common knowledge is the "know-how" rather than the "know-what"—and it is the know-how that is unique to a specific company: "This very specificity is what gives the knowledge gained from experience its potential to provide an organization with a competitive edge."[17]

Dixon argues that organizations must reinvent and update their common knowledge. They achieve this through two different kinds of knowledge activities: "First, they have to find effective ways to translate their ongoing experience into knowledge—create common knowledge. Second, they have to transfer that knowledge across time and space—leverage common knowledge."[18] These processes do not happen automatically; it takes a certain amount of intention to create knowledge out of experience and to transfer (or leverage) knowledge across time and space. In her book, Dixon identifies five types of knowledge transfer that can occur in an organization and suggests ways of facilitating and improving such transfer.

Most important, her research showed that one size does not fit all: "The method that any one organization used to leverage knowledge bore little resemblance to the method that any other organization was using, although each organization seemed to swear by its own process."[19]

However, although there must be diversity of approach, it is possible to discern what makes a method of knowledge transfer effective in a given situation. Dixon expressed her findings in terms of three criteria that determine how a transfer will work in a specific situation: the intended receiver of the knowledge in terms of similarity of task and context; the nature of the task in terms of how routine and frequent it is; the type of knowledge that is being transferred.[20]

The second commentator, Andrew Mayo, has written extensively on training and learning issues. As a former head of personnel at ICL Europe, he is also conscious of the practical problems surrounding implementation. It is his contribution to the learning organization literature that is of particular relevance here. In a well-received book, originally written in 1994 with Elizabeth Lank, a colleague at ICL, he defined the learning organization as follows: "A Learning Organization harnesses the full brainpower, knowledge and experience available to it, in order to evolve continually for the benefit of all its stakeholders."[21] This definition is, to use the word introduced earlier, aspirational. No organization today would claim to harness the full brainpower available to it. What managers (and especially those who carry responsibility for training) can do is to put processes in place to achieve this aim. Where Mayo's analysis is of value is that his approach to the learning organization emphasizes the need for a variety of such processes to be put in place on a consistent basis. His model is presented in diagrammatic form in Figure 3-2.

No organization today would claim to harness the full brainpower available to it.

In his book, Mayo introduces a checklist questionnaire that outlines the steps and issues that must be considered to implement the model. This list embraces the gamut of practical issues that need to be discussed to advance toward the aspirational goal of his definition of the learning organization.

FIGURE 3-2
The complete learning organization.

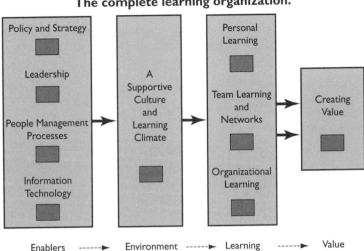

(Reproduced with permission of A. Mayo and E. Lank, *The Power of Learning: A Guide to Gaining Competitive Advantage* [London: Institute of Personnel and Development, 1994].)

The identification of the appropriate practical steps that should be taken to develop competitive advantage through people lies at the heart of the training function. If they are undertaken in a coordinated manner, they could sensibly be defined as promoting organizational learning. There has been much debate (often insufficiently rigorous) in the training profession on organizational learning and the learning organization. This could evaporate and the focus move to a discussion on the practical steps needed to encourage the individual to acquire know-how and to share/leverage it in the organization.

The Learning Organization Revisited

The preceding analysis of the convergence of process and the outline of Nancy Dixon's and Andrew Mayo's refreshingly practical approaches to implementation help to introduce Proposition 8.

Proposition 8

E-learning can give new meaning to the concept of the learning organization.

The underlying suggestion behind Proposition 8 is deceptively simple. Efforts to create a learning organization are characterized by coordinated activities that attempt to foster individual learning. Although this is conceptually straightforward, such activities are demanding in practice. E-learning alters the scope of these activities and makes coordination easier to understand.

A starting point is to return to one of the key themes introduced earlier in this chapter: the value of the distinction between learning and training. To reiterate, the former lies in the domain of the individual, the latter in the domain of the organization.

In the connected economy, information, guidance, and support can be delivered electronically. This has many advantages and, as has been recognized, some limitations. If this delivery is appropriately structured, organized, and supported, it is a powerful enabler for individual learning—this is a definition of effective e-learning.

A learning organization, then, would be one in which the thrust of the organizational training intervention is focused on implementing effective e-learning in the wider cultural context. It would be characterized by the following:

♦ Efforts to inculcate learning in all activities
♦ Acceptance in the culture that learning should take place beyond what is narrowly defined as essential
♦ Training interventions that have, as a matter of course, been designed to encourage the learner to take responsibility and ownership for learning

These characteristics are more properly viewed as a description of the activities involved in creating a learning organization than as a definition of a learning organization. They see the learning organization as an aspirational rather than an absolute concept. They avoid unhelpful debates about whether an organization is or is not a learning organization. They avoid the imprecision of definition that has so often characterized discussions of the concept of the learning organization.

These characteristics also recognize that many individuals themselves will need to make a personal paradigm shift. They will need to recognize that their acceptance of responsibility for their own development is the key to employability. Those charged with increasing the human capital of the organization will need to acquire the skills to help the learner make this attitudinal shift.

Irrespective of the future of the concept of the learning organization, Proposition 9 can be offered with confidence. What it is saying is that in a relatively short time (perhaps two or three years), those involved in training in organizations will have developed a new way of looking at their world. They will share a new conceptual framework in which to construct models and determine practice.

Proposition 9

A new paradigm based on learner-centered interventions will emerge. This will draw on business, learning, and traditional training models.

Connectivity will create a convergence among the different approaches available to gain competitive advantage through people. Together with other technology enablers, it will allow the focus to be placed on the individual learner. It is always dangerous to predict the future—and the impact of the Internet makes it an even more hazardous process. Often the models we use in HR are regarded as absolute when they should be viewed as evolving. We need to be comfortable with uncertainty and a more tentative approach. However, the new paradigm will be characterized by:

♦ Emphasis on the learner and his or her acceptance of responsibility.
♦ A holistic (or integrated) approach to creating competitive advantage through people in the organization
♦ The need to ensure that resources are focused appropriately and managed effectively

The phrase *learner-centered interventions* is offered as a label for this paradigm—with trepidation.

Notes

1   G. M. Piskurich and E. S. Sanders, *ASTD Models for Learning Technologies: Roles, Competencies and Outputs* (Alexandria, Va.: ASTD, 1998).

2   C. Argyris and D. A. Schon, *Organizational Learning: A Theory of Action Perspective* (Wokingham, U.K.: Addison-Wesley, 1978).

3   P. M. Senge, *The Fifth Discipline: The Art and Practice of the Learning Organization* (New York: Doubleday, 1990).

4   Ibid., 12.

5   T. A. Stewart, *Intellectual Capital* (London: Nicholas Brealey, 1997).

6   Ibid., x.

7   S. Davis and C. Meyer, *Future Wealth* (Boston, Mass.: Ernst & Young Center for Business Innovation/Harvard Business School Press, 2000).

8   Ibid.

9   A. Campbell and K. S. Luchs, eds., *Core Competency-Based Strategy* (London: International Thomson Business Press, 1997).

10 I. Nonaka, "The Knowledge-Creating Company," *Harvard Business Review* 69, no. 6 (1991): 96–104.

11 I. Nonaka and H. Taakkeuchi, *The Knowledge-Creating Company: How Japanese Companies Create the Dynamics of Innovation* (Oxford: Oxford University Press, 1993).

12 Nonaka, "The Knowledge-Creating Company," 96–97.

13 H. Scarbrough, J. Swan, and J. Preston, *Knowledge Management: A Literature Review* (London: Institute of Personnel and Development, 1999).

14 Ibid., 4.

15 M. Armstrong and A. Baron, *Performance Management: The New Realities* (London: Institute of Personnel and Development, 1998), 7.

16 N. M. Dixon, *Common Knowledge* (Boston, Mass.: Harvard Business School Press, 2000).

17 Ibid., 11.

18 Ibid., 17.

19 Ibid., 21.

20 Ibid., 22.

21 A. Mayo and E. Lank, *The Power of Learning: A Guide to Gaining Competitive Advantage* (London: Institute of Personnel and Development, 1994), viii.

Chapter 4

Developing the Agenda
for the Organization

"Our similarities are different."

The impact of the connected economy on training extends over all aspects of training activity. The last chapter concluded with the argument that a new paradigm for training will emerge, which was described as learner-centered interventions. It will draw on business, learning, and traditional training models. The challenge is to use the new opportunity presented by connectivity to put the focus on the learners and to define training interventions so as to assist and facilitate their relevant learning. In facing this challenge, all those responsible for training must draw on insights and information from a variety of sources, especially the new business models that have emerged from the arrival of the Internet.

The challenge is to put the focus
on the learners.

To revisit the arguments advanced so far, the connected economy has led to new opportunities in all facets of economic and commercial activity through enhanced communications. More generally, the nature of market competition and the emergence of new business models mean different skills will be required in most organizations. The training sector will be affected as much as other industries. A powerful new platform has emerged: A proportion of training will be delivered through the Internet/intranet using Web-based protocols. The new platform of connectivity will provide a new opportunity for effective training that goes far beyond training design and delivery.

This chapter focuses on action needed at the microlevel. All those charged with the implementation of training are facing tough choices. What should they do in their organization—starting next Monday morning? How should they meet the challenge posed by this disruptive technology? How, most important, can expensive mistakes be avoided?

Although every organization faces different circumstances, some general principles are emerging. These follow from the application of the new Internet business models to the training situation. Focus Point 14 lists principles drawn from the work of Stan Davis and Chris Meyer. The argument, which must be stressed, is that everyone should look at their organization and see what is appropriate. At the same time, they should constantly scan the external environment to seek to identify the opportunities that technology can offer. So far, these opportunities (or best practice) have been realized in the commercial/economic arena, rather than in training.

At the end of this chapter, several case studies are presented. These concern organizations that have drawn up (or are in the process of

---

Focus Point 14: General Principles for Implementing E-Learning

The principles set out here were adapted from a consideration of "50 ways to blur your business," contained in Stan Davis and Chris Meyer's *Blur: The Speed of Change in the Connected Economy*.[1]

♦ *Try to connect everything with everything*—seek information flows with all parties that are involved in the design, delivery, and use of training, whether inside or outside your organization.
♦ *Use different outlets for delivery*—the end user (the learner) will benefit from choice of access.
♦ *Deliver anytime, anywhere and communicate and take feedback online*—give the learners easy access and the power to decide when to learn, and allow them to send feedback.
♦ *Customize your offer to the user and improve it continuously*—tailor your offer to each individual user, letting the user have it on his or her terms.

drawing up) an appropriate agenda for the introduction of e-learning. Those responsible have found it necessary to make what may be called *robust decisions*. These can be described as short-term decisions that carry the organization forward to an agreed objective, but do not prevent the opportunity of proceeding differently if circumstances change (the expression was originally defined by Robert Eccles of Harvard Business School). The pace of recent change, and the fact that the technological platforms available to the trainer are "borrowed" from other uses in the organization, have made life difficult for the training manager. Robust decisions are definitely required.

As will be seen, the organizations in the case studies have used different approaches and are at different stages in their development. They vary in terms of size, objectives, history, and culture. CERN was an early adopter and pioneer in e-learning. Pantex is focusing on the different problems of learner acceptance. Just Born is a smaller organization in the manufacturing sector where, at present, the case for applying e-learning may, at first glance, appear to be less compelling. Some of the training managers in the case studies presented at different stages in this book have adopted a bold and adventurous implementation plan that may carry a degree of risk; others have been tentative and measured. All, however, have paid regard to Proposition 10.

Proposition 10

Training managers should identify the appropriate wins in their organization rather than let the availability of technology determine their agenda.

The key word in Proposition 10 is *appropriate;* in an earlier draft the phrase *easy wins* was used. The appropriate wins may indeed be the easy wins—the initiatives that can be delivered through the existing technology platforms and that demonstrate quickly what e-learning is about. An introduction of a learning portal would be a good example. However, the appropriate choice could be something that is seen to bring real value to the organization in achieving its wider objectives. Giving an internal subject matter expert the capability to author Web-based training is an example of an entirely appropriate win that may be far from easy. This compromise between easy (by implication quick and cheap) and high value (by implication expensive and demanding) seems to run as an undercurrent in the thoughts of the training managers interviewed in the course of the case studies.

The discussions with the case study training managers in the United States and Europe offered a further insight. Those managers who seemed likely to succeed, or at least less likely to stumble into costly mistakes, had one feature in common. When asked to outline the purpose of their e-learning intervention, they invariably described it in terms of a critical business objective or mission. For Pantex it is the need to meet stringent safety requirements; for Ernst & Young it is the need to offer a consistent global service to global clients. This does not mean that the path for organizations will be smooth. However, the clear business focus (as opposed to a learning initiative for its own sake) will mean that a wider coalition of support will be secured across the organization and that problems are more likely to be overcome.

When the earlier edition of this book appeared in the United Kingdom, I received numerous telephone inquiries from training managers seeking advice. These were welcome but some sounded alarm bells. These began with "I want to get into e-learning. How should I go about it?" At a time of disruptive technology, this is a risky mind-set. Doubtless similar thoughts went through people's minds when other significant innovations arrived. At the onset of the railway did ambitious individuals ask, "How do I get into this new transport thing?" rather than "Where do I want to get to and why?"

Cost and Budget

One of the most critical factors affecting the ability to make robust decisions is the need for a cost estimate. Given the speed of change, it would be misleading to offer any hard and fast guidance. Remember, Moore's Law states that every eighteen months computer-processing power doubles while cost holds constant.

Any estimates I have provided will be out of date by the time this book goes to print. Some figures were offered in a few of the case studies, but these reflect the particular approach used by that organization at that time.

One approach to cost estimation is to assume that up to a quarter of the training volume will be delivered using technology. Training delivered through this means will be cheaper; this is often seen as the main justification. A rough estimate of ongoing costs per user at, say, 10 percent of training budget could be set for the initial forays into the e-learning arena—if a piecemeal rather than a big bang approach is to be adopted.

A significant point to emerge from this hypothetical discussion is that the nature of the investment decision has changed. The traditional resourcing decision facing the training manager was straightforward: A course was costed; budgets were set on the basis of the cost of the courses offered on the training menu. Depending on the organization, the costs could be charged back to individual users or their departments. Budget pressure would lead to courses being withdrawn from the menu.

In e-learning, a different sort of investment decision is required. It is a project decision: An initial investment is required that will lead to ongoing savings in future years. Fortunately, there is considerable experience in the IT departments of such project costing—it is to them that the training manager must look for guidance and advice.

Single Frames

Single frames can assist in the process of making robust decisions. To recapitulate, a single frame is a diagram on one page that captures key concepts in graphic form. A major advantage of single frames is that they can form the basis of a useful exchange and dialogue. This occurs when they are completed in conjunction with another party; summary phrases are inserted in the empty boxes as an outcome of a focused meeting. Ernst & Young has developed the single frame as an approach to client relationships. Exactly the same principle applies to relationships with internal clients.

Several single frames are presented next. In each case, it is recommended that the training manager seek advice inside and outside the organization and complete the relevant text.

The first two single frames are presented as Figures 4-1 and 4-2. They are, respectively, an e-learning transformation matrix and an instrument for defining the e-learning solution that is appropriate to the organization. They are offered to the reader to use as he or she wishes, but with a firm recommendation that other stakeholders in the organization be involved. Remember, single frames can form the basis of a useful exchange and dialogue.

Figure 4-1 simply recasts the Ernst & Young transformation matrix introduced in Chapter 1. The argument was that specific initiatives were needed to transform organizations to become an e-business and that four stages in this transformation could be identified. Figure 4-1 expresses this transformation in training or learning terms. The column headings describe the stages of the transformation. The headings next to the rows identify four key activities undertaken by those responsible for training.

FIGURE 4-1
E-learning transformation matrix.

	Transformation			
	E-Information (accessing and delivering through an electronic channel)	E-Exchange (formal and quantified entry and exchange of learning opportunities)	E-Delivery (identification and delivery of services using an intranet)	E-Training (connections with all aspects of corporate development strategies; permeable boundaries with external learning opportunities)
Needs identification				
Sources of training solutions				
Delivery of training				
Management of resources				

FIGURE 4-2

Defining the e-learning solution.

New business model for the organization (how will the organization compete in the connected economy?)	

Marketplace (how do users gain information on learning opportunities?)	
Customer connections (how does the market clear?)	
Supply chain (how is design and delivery organized?)	

Figure 4-2 reflects some of the principles set out in Focus Point 14. It reinforces the argument that training is a market just like any other. For example, the question, "How does the market clear?" asks the training manager to consider how learning resources are actually allocated to the learner. Does a price mechanism operate (such as by charging for courses against departmental budgets), or is supply and demand applied in another way (such as by compulsory training)?

In all transmissions to the learner, a value chain is involved.

Figure 4-2 also reintroduces the term *supply chain*. This was defined in Chapter 1 as "a system whose constituent parts include material suppliers, production facilities, distribution services, and customers linked via the forward flow of materials and the forward and backward flow of information." When the term was introduced, it was argued that the Internet would have a significant effect on the value or supply chain. Although the term *supply chain* is more common (supply chain management is a well-explored and well-recognized process), in many ways the term *value chain* is preferable. Training managers do not instinctively think in terms of the value chain, but in all transmissions to the learner (the end consumer), a value chain is involved. Given the increasing blur caused by the Internet, the term *value Web* (rather than value chain) is starting to be used. This emphasizes the importance of different contributions and varying relationships at all stages of transmission.

An outline value chain is shown diagrammatically in Figure 4-3. It is important for those responsible for training to consider the chain that applies in their organization. The Internet will, with certainty, affect that value chain and offer new opportunities. There are often significant transaction costs for each of the components of the value chain, and the Internet (through the market effect; see Focus Point 5) will force greater efficiency. This is summarized in Proposition 11.

Proposition 11

Training professionals should investigate the new business models. They should review their value chains.

FIGURE 4-3
The supply or value chain.

A generic model

How it might appear to the training manager

What is the training content — the building blocks of knowledge and skill elements? Who creates or supplies them?	How are the building blocks put together into a cohesive module or program? Is this done in-house or outsourced?	How are the modules or programs delivered? Are they courses, technology-based training, or experiential events?	How are the end users made aware of the events? How do they access them?	What support does the end user (the learner) need and how is it delivered? What is the reinforcement of learning (the after-sales service)?

Raw Materials → Manufacturing → Distribution → Marketing → Customer

The E-Learning Agenda

The next single frame, Figure 4-4, is a general tool that could be applied in a host of situations and in organizations that are at very different stages in their thinking. The tool should be of interest to all responsible for developing HR, but especially to the training manager.

The top half of Figure 4-4 offers the training manager an opportunity to map the current and desired future states and to identify the major enablers and blockages. The left-hand box (current state) suggests that a simple SWOT (strengths, weaknesses, opportunities, threats) analysis should be conducted, preferably in conjunction with other people outside the training department. The middle box looks at the future state. What is the preferred relationship between training and the business? How can training as a whole add value? Given this relationship, how should the training department be structured and how should its role be defined?

The right-hand box contains a list of key issues that need to be considered at the beginning of the transition to e-learning. The first

FIGURE 4-4
Determining your e-training agenda.

Current State		Future State	Key Issues
Strengths	Weaknesses	Training and the business	State of technology
			Intranet/extranet
			Training delivery to date
			Learning support
Opportunities	Threats	Structure and role of the training department	Coaching capability
			Awareness of training suppliers

E-Training Options	
Protect the core	Change the game
Current Initiatives Future Initiatives	Current Initiatives Future Initiatives

two (the state of technology and intranet/extranet) demand a discussion with those responsible for IT in the organization. It is a self-evident proposition that any e-training initiative:

♦ Should not put an unacceptable load on the network and services
♦ Should be consistent and compatible with other developments

The next key issues (training delivery to date, learning support, coaching capability, and awareness of training suppliers) invite consideration of the current pattern of delivery and the opportunity for change. As will be argued in the next chapter, the introduction of e-learning will focus attention on some of the softer aspects of training. The concept of learning support will be developed more fully later (see Chapter 5), and coaching will be a key element in that provision.

The bottom half of Figure 4-4 invites decisions. The options can be divided into two strategies. One is to protect the core. The strategy here is to do enough to maintain the position of training in the organization. What steps or initiatives need to be taken now and in the future to ensure that training does not become marginalized (or even abolished)? This may sound defensive, but for some the threat may be real. When technology-based training was in its early stages, an overreliance on CBT undoubtedly led to a failure to recognize some positive aspects of face-to-face training. For some organizations and individuals, the consequences would have been dire.

The alternative strategy is labeled "Change the game." At its boldest this means that the training manager will seek a rapid transformation based on e-learning. He or she will seek different relationships in the organization, based on different methods of delivery, and earn new respect, possibly resulting in leading-edge status in the profession. Such a course, while it may be for only the bold, should always be considered and its consequences assessed. If not, some easy short-term gains could be overlooked.

Is Technology Necessarily the Best Course?

So far the frameworks and approaches outlined in this chapter have assumed a general acceptance of the value of e-learning: that it is beneficial and, indeed, that its advance is inevitable.

But you can't replace the classroom experience.

To many decision makers in organizations, however, the proposition is far from self-evident. Such sentiments will be shared by those in the training community who have not been exposed to the potential of Internet/intranet-based approaches. The objection is often expressed as, "But you can't replace the classroom experience."

This objection should not be dismissed lightly. It has much substance. It was also given much credence by experience with previous generations of CBT. The improved delivery offered by the CD-ROM was often pushed beyond its sensible limits, and some restricted soft-skills training (even extending to assertiveness skills) was offered as a substitute to course-based personal interaction. This problem continues as WBT is oversold by organizations and individuals who do not always demonstrate an appreciation of the principles underlying effective learning.

For most people who have explored the opportunities created by the new technology platforms, the argument has moved beyond this stage. The potential of e-learning is enormous, but it must be introduced in an appropriate structure. Proposition 12, therefore, would command general support.

Proposition 12

E-learning will be most effective for the acquisition of knowledge and least effective where interpersonal interaction is needed for learning.

Recall that the ASTD survey outlined in Chapter 2 quoted a figure of 22 percent for training delivered through the intranet. By general recognition, Motorola is considered one of the most sophisticated organizations in terms of its approach to e-learning (see Chapter 5 for a case study based on its experience). Motorola's target for training delivered through alternative (nonclassroom) means was 30 percent for 2000, rising to 50 percent by 2003.

Even on the most bullish of estimates, there will continue to be a high proportion of training delivered by nontechnological means. There will continue to be a balance among different approaches. What is important is that this balance be considered and planned appropriately.

No matter how sophisticated an organization is, e-learning should never be introduced in isolation, as Proposition 13 suggests. The phrase *experiential learning* needs some explanation: It refers to the activities that support an individual's ongoing development. Mentoring, coaching, action learning, and self-managed learning are all examples. Here, the individual learns through experience, but the organization intervenes to create or support that experience.

Proposition 13

E-learning will be most effective as part of a systematic approach involving classroom and experiential learning with appropriate support.

Much of the background discussion to support this proposition is presented in the next chapter, which focuses firmly on the learner. The bias to the classroom is explored further and issues of learner preferences and support for learning are considered. These are some of the component issues to be considered in what is now described as *blended learning,* now accepted as the term to describe the desirable future. E-learning will be most effective when it is part of an overall strategy involving the classroom and on-the-job workplace learning. It will be most effective when the learner is given comprehensive and timely support. This support will range from initial guidance on the use of technology, through to the creation of online communities to share ideas—never, of course, neglecting the social interaction gained through face-to-face contact.

Given the analysis presented so far, and in this chapter in particular, blended learning is an eminently sensible concept. The problem is moving beyond a recognition of the importance of a blended approach to implementation in practice. HR is littered with concepts in search of an application.

Former U.S. Labor Secretary Robert Reich made the following quip: "Rarely has a term moved so rapidly from obscurity to meaninglessness without passing through an intervening period of coherence." However he somewhat ruined the effect by using the phrase twice in a four-month period, first at the OECD Conference in Paris to describe flexibility, then at the National Alliance of Business in Dallas to describe competitiveness.[2]

The challenge for the profession is to ground the concept of blended learning in reality. One can expect a plethora of articles and conference papers on the subject over the next few years. At present, the term *blended learning* is aspirational and imprecise, but some patterns are emerging. One observation is that the term is being used in two, by no means mutually exclusive, senses.

In the first application of the term, the blend concentrates on the subject or content matter. The purpose of the blend is to ensure that the right topic is delivered using the right medium. Simplistically, soft skills require the facilitated classroom and role-play practice; information-rich content can be dispatched in print form or via the Internet. In a second application of the term, the blend is seen as a sequencing process. Internet delivery precedes classroom delivery in a structured and considered manner. The IBM Global E-Learning Model, which formed the second case study in Chapter 2, offers a good example of blended learning as appropriate sequencing. Whatever approach is adopted, blended learning must meet the needs of the learner. Chapter 5 takes us into a more detailed consideration of what might be involved in achieving this aim.

The goal of this chapter was twofold. First, it sought to demystify e-learning. Progress is not about buying a learning system; it is about identifying the appropriate solution for the organization and making robust decisions. Second, it offered a series of instruments (known as single frames) that provide a framework for discussion in the reader's own organization. Ultimately, the reader must carry the responsibility of progressing the debate.

The following case studies illustrate the diverse approaches that are being adopted by thoughtful HR professionals. My thanks to them for their willingness to share their experiences with others.

Notes

1   S. Davis and C. Meyer, *Blur: The Speed of Change in the Connected Economy* (Oxford: Ernst & Young/Center for Business Innovation/Capstone, 1998).

2   I am grateful to Warren S. Sinsheimer for drawing my attention to the double use of this quotation.

CERN

CERN is the European Organization for Nuclear Research (otherwise known as the European Laboratory for Particle Physics), established in 1953 to:

> provide for collaboration among European States in nuclear research of a pure scientific and fundamental character and in research essentially related thereto. The organization shall have no concern with work for military requirements and the results of its experimental and practical work shall be published.

CERN (an independent international organization pre-dating the European Union) provides its member states with the facilities to carry out research into the basic structure of matter and the fundamental laws of nature via high-energy particle accelerators and detectors. The UK was a founding member of CERN and remains very actively involved through many university physics departments, the Rutherford Appleton Laboratory (RAL), and the Particle Physics and Astronomy Research Council (PPARC).

Over nearly the next half-century, the fundamental objectives—collaboration among scientists in leading-edge particle physics—remain unchanged. However, this collaboration has extended beyond Europe to the rest of the world (*http://public.web.cern.ch/Public/Welcome.html*). CERN is now the leading world laboratory in this field, with active participation from countries such as the United States, Japan, Russia, China, and India, as well as from its member states.

Most interestingly, from the point of view of this book, the World Wide Web was born at CERN as a vehicle to allow data for scientific research to be shared across boundaries.

CERN now embraces a network of some 10,000 people. The headquarters is at a large site in Geneva and employs approximately 2,700 people, with another 600 on short-term assignments. CERN employs very few research physicists directly, since the research is conducted primarily by physicists in universities and national institutes throughout Europe and, indeed, the world. CERN employees are engineers, applied physicists, computer specialists and technicians, plus administrative support staff. Evidently, and this has been shaped by CERN's approach to learning and development, they are mainly knowledge workers who are generally confident with technology and its uses. In addition, there are 6,000 people who share their time between their home university and CERN, and another 1,000 who perform some outsourced activities on the CERN site. The entire network is eligible to access and take advantage of CERN's training provision.

CERN was a comparatively early entrant into e-learning. Two developments, WBT and a current research and education initiative, are of particular interest.

Web-Based Training
CERN has invested in training that is delivered to the desktop via the Internet. This approach aims to provide:

♦ Just-in-time training for people who are not able to wait for an instructor-led course

- Precourse support for people who wish to start learning a subject before they start an instructor-led course
- Postcourse reference material for people who need to review topics they have learned in an instructor-led course
- Structured learning material for people who do not have time to follow an instructor-led course
- Learning material presented in easy-to-review modules for people who want to decide whether they need to follow an instructor-led course

For a small cost (far less than the cost of access to CERN's course-based training), participants can get unlimited access to a full set of courses from the suppliers NETg and Ziff Davis.

The original pilot of WBT took place in 1998, with more testing in 1999 before a decision to commit was made. A dedicated NETg server has been installed, and Ziff Davis packages are accessed through the supplier's own server in the United States. This provides the added value of supplying immediate access to new course offerings as they are published and avoids maintenance overheads.

CERN is confident that this approach has resulted in value for both the organization and the individual. However, resources have not permitted CERN to give the marketing support it feels the initiative deserves. "These things don't fly by themselves." Furthermore, CERN would also like to have more time to devote to an analysis of the usage statistics generated by the two systems. This would lead to a more fundamental evaluation of impact.

CERN has, however, more than enough information to convince it that this is an appropriate form of training for the right person. In the words of Mick Storr, CERN's head of technical training:

> Training delivered to the desktop via the Web is attractive for certain types of people. It appeals to: those with an academic bent, people who have been through university, people who are used to learning and used to teaching themselves. For people for whom

the computer is an obstacle, this approach is bound to be less useful.

WBT has not resulted in the elimination of course-based training but fills an important gap for an extended community. It is likely to become increasingly important in the training of new staff members and will complement course-based training. As Bill Blair, head of the training and development group, puts it: "It releases time and resources to allow us to produce better instructor-led programs."

Accessing Seminar Resource Information

CERN's technical e-learning project initially concentrated on access to content obtained through two suppliers. The Ziff Davis content allows participants to join chat rooms and instructor-led virtual training, but such excursions by CERN participants have been limited. CERN has not sought to author or customize content. Instead, it has developed a second and complementary strand of e-learning designed to exploit and promote its rich in-house academic and technical seminar programs.

CERN is currently collaborating with the University of Michigan in a venture designed to capture and catalog seminars for playback via the Web, including full video, audio, and visual support material using minimal (less than 56 kbaud) bandwidth requirements. This means that these seminars will be accessible to anyone worldwide with a typical home modem using standard Web browsers and free publicly available video playback software. A significant number of recordings have already been made and can be viewed, along with details of the project (*http://webcast.cern.ch/ Projects/WebLectureArchive/index.html*).

The project is now being extended to investigate the potential of asynchronous virtual classrooms. The barriers surrounding intellectual property must be resolved before these techniques can be exploited for dissemination of commercial course offerings.

Overview

CERN is unusually well placed to introduce WBT. Organizationally, it shares knowledge among staff who are computer literate and are likely to be self-motivated. The CERN HR and training professionals see many possibilities for extension—even with the existing technology infrastructure. They, however, emphatically emphasize the need for more resource support if maximum leverage and value is to be gained. In the words of Blair:

> Web-based training is an exciting addition to the menu of training methods. For some people with the appropriately disciplined mindset it could fulfill almost all their training needs. However, the temptation to suppress other forms of training and give staff unassisted access to a vast library of Web-based courses should be avoided. Key factors in the successful use of Web-based courses are:

♦ *Complementarity*—Web-based training is best used as a complement to other forms of training

♦ *Effectiveness*—there should be prior assessment of the suitability of the Web-based course(s) for the organization and for the individual, and then ongoing evaluation of the progress achieved by individuals using Web-based learning

♦ *Resources*—adequate resources should be allocated both for the initial assessment and then for marketing and support for the Web-based training operation

♦ *"Nous"*—flair and knowledge of the culture of the organization help a lot in identifying training needs and appropriate Web-based courses to meet these needs, and above all, in delivering results

Complete information on CERN's training programs is available at *http://public.web.cern.ch/Public/TRAINING/eduintro.html.*

Author's Note: My thanks to Bill Blair and Mick Storr for their assistance in the preparation of this case study.

PANTEX

The Pantex Plant in Amarillo, Texas, is the nation's sole facility for maintaining and dismantling its nuclear weapons stockpile, with nearly 3,000 employees on one site. Pantex is in a highly regulated environment overseen by federal, state, and local agencies. Continuing training is important in ensuring a safe and qualified workforce.

In 1992, Pantex began to convert many of the basic compliance courses (those required by federal law or by the Department of Energy) from classroom-based training to CBT courses accessible through PCs. These courses are required by all employees from the yard worker to the general manager. Implementing this process required Pantex to overcome human and technical problems.

Turnover at Pantex at 3 percent per year is very low, which created one of the initial hurdles for e-learning. The average age of the employees is 48, so there were a lot of people who were not comfortable with computers. Converting classroom courses to CBT was intimidating for them. Design issues had to be solved in terms of computer literacy, navigation architecture, student feedback, and interaction.

The nature of the work and size of the plant also created problems. Pantex has jobs ranging from janitorial work requiring only an eighth-grade reading level to scientists and engineers with Ph.D.s who design and develop nuclear weapons and high explosives. Many of the compliance courses are required for every worker at the plant, so creating products that would not overwhelm some of the workforce or bore others was a challenge.

Nearly half the workforce is unionized, particularly production technicians, crafts personnel, and security forces. Getting union management buy-in and support was also critical to success.

Technical issues included selecting and acquiring the right hardware and software for developing and implementing in-house-developed courseware. Because much of the work is classified, most courses and CBT are developed in-house. Distribution of CBT to a large population, nearly half of whom had no access to computers, was yet another problem.

Overcoming the Problems

Early mistakes were made. Far too much time was taken in an effort to produce the best possible initial product. Funding for the program was almost withdrawn because it took nearly eighteen months to acquire the equipment, hire and train the developers, and launch the first product. In retrospect, Everett Poore, training manager, believes that to get e-learning off the ground, "You need to get something relatively simple that shows returns on investment as quick as possible."

Furthermore, the project manager had a graphic arts background and decided that MacIntosh computers would be the best development platform. However, the plant standard was IBM PC–compatible computers. This forced Pantex into selecting a courseware development software that claimed to allow the development of programs on the MacIntosh that could be converted into PC format. This process failed miserably. Pantex was never able to successfully convert Mac-based courses to PC-based platforms and had to abandon the use of Macs entirely.

To overcome the computer illiteracy of much of the plant population, online tutorials were built for activities as basic as how to use a mouse. All courses offered the tutorials for any employee needing help. Buttons were made large and easy to read and included audio feedback when clicked. The navigation architecture for courses was standardized so that each was used exactly the same way. The problem arising from diversity in ages, computer skills, education, and other factors was overcome by adding numerous graphics, humor, and other touches to increase the entertainment value of the courses. Additionally, test-out options were offered for individuals who already knew the information and did not need to page through screen after screen of information they already knew.

To reach plant employees with no access to computers, Pantex created eleven CBT learning centers plantwide, each with an assigned proctor. Employees can go to the nearest learning center to complete their training. Additionally, one of the learning centers is located at the union office, which allows union personnel the more comfortable option of having other union personnel help them to use computers. Moreover, the union president and stewards were invited to test courses as they came online. By doing so, any complaints concerning fears about using computers were quelled because the union officers could say that they had already taken the courses and found them easy to use and understand.

The Outcomes

Although Pantex had selected its software based on the wrong assumption, it turned out that the chosen software permitted a more powerful program, so the test-out option could become part of the program. This programming strength later helped Pantex convert CD-based CBT courseware into intranet-delivered courses that employees can take at their desktops, although half of all employees do not have access to computers (and some of those with intranet access elect to use a learning center instead to avoid distractions).

With intranet delivery, the previous forty-two delivery systems taking three days to reload are now combined in one, which takes half an hour. There is a measurable savings in time as well, since employees do not have to walk to and from learning centers at the plant. The new system also allows the courses to be presented in a test-out format. When people log in to take their required courses, instead of starting with the first screen of the course, they start with the first test question for that course. If they answer it correctly, they can either review the material or proceed to the next test question. If they ignore the question, or give a wrong answer, they receive relevant learning materials and must provide the correct answer before they can proceed to the next learning objective. Employees without access to a PC at their workplace take their training at one of the learning centers.

When Pantex first moved to CBT, it invested $400,000 over the first eighteen months in equipment and resources, including four CBT developers and managers. Break-even point arrived after about three years. The company estimates that four and a half days of classroom training translates into four and a half hours of

CBT. On a total training budget of $4.5 million, CBT means an annual savings of about $850,000, taking into account two software developers employed at about $150,000.

Pantex needs a minimum of 300 employees to justify the costs of preparing CBT materials, and 70 percent of all training is still delivered face-to-face. In 2000, there were 282,000 hours of contact time. Initial training and advanced technical training are still virtually all classroom based—when it comes to dismantling a bomb, it doesn't seem worth taking the risk of someone hitting the right button by chance on a multiple-choice question! With 3,000 employees, every forty-five minutes saved by training through the new technologies translates into a person-year of training time.

The Future
Everett Poore believes that Pantex now provides as much e-learning as possible. The challenge for the future, with much of the safety training repeating what has been covered in previous years, is to find more amusing and entertaining ways of presenting "the same tired old stuff."

Author's Note: My thanks to Everett Poore for his assistance in the preparation of this case study.

JUST BORN

Just Born is a seventy-seven-year-old confectionery company located in Bethlehem, Pennsylvania (readers may recognize Marshmallow Peeps, Mike & Ikes, Teenie Beanies, Zours, and Hot Tamales, to name a few of their products). It is privately held and owned by the second and third generation of the original family. The company has approximately 475 employees and a turnover of approximately 2 percent.

Because most of Just Born's employees are on-site, using e-learning for staff training was not an obvious approach. The company decided to invest in e-learning for several reasons. First, it wanted to make opportunities for learning and training available to employees on all three shifts. Second, it wanted to provide access to training opportunities even when there was only a small group of people (perhaps working different shifts) who would participate. Finally, the company has regional sales managers around the country and it wanted to make learning opportunities available to them as well.

History of the Initiative

Just Born began working on its e-learning initiative in 1999. As a centralized, midsize company, it was decided that the company would begin by bringing in training modules from an outside supplier, rather than developing its own modules. The project was initiated by the training team but was strongly backed by the executive team, which also comprises the "training council" that evaluates proposals and plans for training initiatives and how training is assessed within the company. Meloney Sallie-Dosunmu, employee relations and development manager at Just Born, describes the executive team as very supportive largely because a key component of the company's overall strategic plan is to enhance organizational effectiveness.

E-learning is a joint initiative between the training and the IT departments. Subject matter falls into two key areas: business skills and IT. A training coordination team is made up of representatives from IT, operations, and HR to coordinate strategic training issues within the company. The e-learning initiative was developed in tandem with the relaunch of a company learning center in April 2001.

Sallie-Dosunmu says, "Like every training professional I was inundated with offers from e-learning providers," but Just Born made a conscious decision to "start small." She compiled a list of criteria:

♦ Good-quality learning experience with sound content and engaging delivery

◆ Pay by use, not availability
◆ Good-quality courses
◆ Low cost
◆ Content mainly consisting of software and business skills
◆ A package of courses that were not so numerous as to be confusing
◆ Intranet and Internet access to courses
◆ A pre- and posttest component to e-learning modules so that progress could be monitored

At the end of the proposal process, Just Born chose USchool as its main provider for software and business skills, and Workplace Essentials for basic skills and GED preparation. Workplace Essentials, a community services program, offers courses free of charge through the State of Pennsylvania's Department of Education. USchool's training modules are mainly general office software but also include forty modules for business skills such as time management, grammar, and project management. Costs are between $55 and $115 for each course category, which are three to fourteen hours long. However, many users dip in and out of courses to learn specific "bite-sized" skills as needed. Software and business skills modules are tracked for usage and evaluation purposes. Workplace Essentials, however, is not tracked in order to maintain privacy for the users, who may feel embarrassed about needing to update basic skills.

Challenges and Problems
Awareness and Access
Because the e-learning initiative was rolled out with the learning center promotion, it suffered in terms of employee awareness by being lost in the shuffle of the many other new learning initiatives introduced at that time. Susan Plate, a member of the Just Born training department, has since established a monthly program to promote the various learning initiatives; the training team hopes that the e-learning program will benefit from this more focused push. Just Born's goal is to provide a learning environment that is most convenient for each person. For some, this may mean that they will learn at their desks. For others, particularly those working on the shop floor, special learning kiosks have been set aside

within the learning center and at other central locations within the premises. These kiosks are available twenty-four hours a day so that all shift workers have access. More kiosks may be added as demand grows. Making the courses accessible from employees' homes encourages learning. For example, many plant-based employees register and get set up for a course at work and then complete it at home.

Another access issue was how employees would use the access. Since the kiosks are located in the learning center and in private areas of the hallways, Just Born had to consider providing access to the Web-based learning without providing access to inappropriate Web sites. This was achieved through close collaboration with the IT department. Each individual has to sign a usage agreement when getting his or her password for Web-based learning. This usage agreement outlines the company policy on Internet use and what types of Web sites are not to be visited on company equipment. The IT department has also installed filtering software to eliminate the possibility of employees using the Web access to visit inappropriate sites.

Technical Problems

There are pros and cons to outsourcing the courseware. On the positive side, outsourcing means that internal time and resources do not need to be used, but the flip side is that there may be no ready support when things go wrong. Also, with so much reliance on the vendor, it is crucial that the vendor be stable and e-learning be its core product. The vendor also has to be ready to quickly address any technical problems. "The technical problems were frustrating," says Sallie-Dosunmu "because if the early users—the pioneers—have difficulties, others won't be encouraged to try e-learning." Although there had been a pilot of the initiative, not all of the technical difficulties were caught. If she had the chance to do it again, Sallie-Dosunmu says she would expand the pilot to include participants with more diverse PC skills. A two-tier pilot would include a highly skilled, desk-based group that could iron out any obvious kinks. Then, the second level of the pilot could be rolled out to a more diverse control group that would include frontline and shop-floor employees. She would also invest in more targeted promotion before the rollout of the e-learning program.

The Future

Just Born hopes to be able to offer a customized product knowledge e-learning module for employee orientation. This will be expensive to develop, so the aim for now is to establish firmly the current offerings, getting more user buy-in and participation before further investment.

Because Just Born has very low employee turnover, it is difficult to justify big spending on e-learning as a recruitment and retention tool. Therefore, it is crucial that the e-learning initiative justify its costs in productivity gains, making evaluation and proof of return on investment important. The main challenge for Just Born will continue to be to find cost-effective ways of delivering learning to all of its employees.

Author's Note: My thanks to Meloney Sallie-Dosunmu, employee relations and development manager at Just Born in Bethlehem, Pennsylvania, for her assistance in the preparation of this case study.

Chapter 5

Focusing on the Learner

"It's déjà vu all over again."

This chapter considers the issues involved in learner support in the age of e-learning. The central argument that runs throughout this consideration is summarized in Proposition 14.

Proposition 14

A new discipline of learner support will emerge and should be encouraged.

The change in emphasis from training to learning was considered in Chapter 3 and should be recognized as marking a major shift in focus for the training professional. Improvements in technology, and particularly the emergence of connectivity, offer the trainer an unprecedented opportunity to deliver interventions that are designed around the needs of the learner. In the vocabulary of Internet business, these can become customer-centric offerings. The learning experience can be tailored to the individual learner's requirements and preferences. The importance of this change in emphasis cannot be overstated. It has led to the emergence of the new paradigm of learner-centered interventions introduced in Chapter 3.

"It's déjà vu all over again" fits this chapter because, to an extent, we are revisiting old territory; we are asking how we can encourage and assist people to learn. There is a considerable body of research and extensive literature on this subject, and some of the most important strands are reviewed later in this chapter. This material is quite theoretical and will prove more demanding for the reader than much of the discussion so far. It is an aspect of the potential of e-learning that will take us nearer to the boundaries of what is known.

There is a danger of being seduced by the technology.

These conceptual frameworks for learning must, however, be considered in the next context. So far, it has been suggested that a quarter of training content could be provided through e-learning. This must necessarily alter the approach to learner support required in the organization. Many of the practical issues of implementation are considered in Chapter 6. To set the scene, the place of learner support is illustrated in Figure 5-1.[1] It portrays the intervention that a trainer makes in the organization as three corners of a triangle. Learning needs should continue to be the starting point; nothing has changed here. The second apex—the platform for delivery—has been dramatically affected by the new technology, which offers exciting opportunities. Regrettably, to date, most of the debate has concentrated on these opportunities; to reemphasize the point made in Proposition 4, there is a danger of being seduced by the technology. It is the opportunity for improved learning that the technology creates that is important. If these exciting opportunities are to be realized, appropriate support for the learner is needed. These issues, described as learner support and outlined at the third and lowest point of the triangle in Figure 5-1, form the subject of this chapter.

A new term is introduced here to describe some of the activities involved in learner support, *soft technology,* and is outlined in Focus Point 15.[2] It can be seen that a broad definition of soft technology is proposed, which is used for the remainder of the book. At its narrowest, the definition could refer to the architecture of the learning material (or how easy it is to navigate and assimilate information). The definition adopted will extend to wider organizational issues, including steps taken to promote, encourage, and facilitate access.

By using this wide definition, appropriate soft technology is required to implement the exciting opportunities created by the hard technol-

FIGURE 5-1
Issues in e-learning.

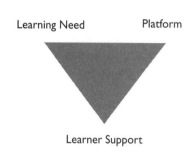

Learning Need   Platform

Learner Support

Learning Need —This should drive the whole process, but new business models have produced a new agenda and new training needs. Identifying training needs remains critical.

Platform — The new technology offers an exciting platform, particularly when used in conjunction with course-based training and experiential learning.

Learner Support — (Coaching, mentoring, etc.) must be supplied appropriately. It will be affected by both learning needs and technology. Adequate provision of learner support is the responsibility of the learning and development profession.

ogy. Learner support describes the activities undertaken by the HR professional to ensure that people learn effectively. In the next chapter, it is argued that the underlying skill set will redefine the roles of many trainers. In this chapter, we consider some of the issues involved in learner support. Be warned: The news is not always good. It is possible to identify many of the questions, but so far the profession has come up with few of the answers.

Connectivity and the Classroom

A useful starting point in identifying some of the significant issues involved in learning in the new context is to ask what is special about classroom learning. Learners and trainers instinctively opt for this method of instruction, certainly for interpersonal skills training. Pete Weaver, senior vice president of the management development consultancy Development Dimensions International, has offered an analysis, reproduced as Focus Point 16.

The arrival of the mobile phone is the biggest assault to date on the training room.

Focus Point 15: Soft Technology

The concept of soft technology is one that is emerging in speeches, commentary, and literature. In April 1999, for example, Sir John Daniel, vice chancellor of the UK Open University, attributed much of the university's success to soft technology. He included the following outline in a speech:

> The key technology for the mega-universities is not any particular device. It is the increasingly organized body of knowledge called distance education. *Distance education uses a combination of hard and soft technologies. Hard technologies are bits and bytes, electrons and pixels, satellites and search engines. Soft technologies are processes, approaches, sets of rules and models of organizations.* [Italics added] The most important thing to understand about using distance education for university-level teaching and learning that is both intellectually powerful and competitively cost-effective is that you must concentrate on getting the soft technologies right. The hard technologies change. Indeed, they change rapidly.

> These soft technologies are simply the working practices that underpin the rest of today's modern and industrial service economy: division of labor, specialization, teamwork and project management. [*www.open.ac.uk/vcs-speeches*]

The important issue here is the valuable distinction between hard and soft technology. This is used throughout the book in the following sense: Hard technology refers to the information and communication technology systems. Figure 2-2 considered the architecture of these systems as applied to learning. Soft technology refers to the activities that must be taken at all levels in an organization to embed that hard technology effectively.

All of Weaver's points have some resonance for the training manager. In addition, getting people together in a classroom can have cultural benefits for the organization. They learn from each other and can gain reassurance from the fact that they face the same problems. Unfortunately, the improved communications associated with the connected economy does diminish the third point in Focus Point 16: separation from interruptions. Unless my experience is unique, the arrival of the mobile phone is the biggest assault to date on the

---

Focus Point 16: A Bias for the Classroom?

♦ *People are social learners*—they enjoy an exchange of ideas with others and like the support of other learners.

♦ *Some people need learning tension*—people often go to classroom events (and remain there) because their absence is conspicuous. However, with e-learning the feeling of anonymity is often commensurate with a lack of commitment.

♦ *There is a separation from interruptions*—if people are in the classroom the primary focus of their activity is clear, and colleagues and subordinates are less likely to offer distractions.

♦ *There is a change in atmosphere*—not only is there a release from telephone interruptions but it is possible to create a mood that is less frenetic and is conducive to reflection.

♦ *There is a sense of self-worth*—in many instances being sent away on a course is seen as an indication that an organization is willing to invest in an individual.

♦ *There is a management bias*—senior managers understand the financial model involved in classroom training. E-learning (with its heavy upfront investment) does not command the same support. The Web has led managers to expect content to be free.

Author's Note: My thanks to Pete Weaver for permission to reproduce his work (*www.ddiworld.com*).

---

training room, with Internet access through hotel switchboards a close second. The imminent convergence of mobile telephones and the Internet is to be dreaded greatly by classroom instructors.

E-learning cannot replicate all the facets that make classroom training popular.

Connectivity, therefore, can be regarded as both a threat and an opportunity for effective organizational learning. The main thrust of this chapter is that it is the training professional's responsibility to understand what is at issue in his or her organization. How do individuals learn what they need or wish to learn? This question can be answered in two ways: first, by gaining a theoretical grounding and considering preferences, styles, and motivation; and, second, by continually gathering information from learning in the organization. What should be gained from this brief overview of the classroom is that e-learning cannot (certainly at present) replicate all the facets that make classroom training popular and well-established.

Frameworks in Training and Education

Marcy Driscoll, professor of Instructional Systems and Educational Psychology at Florida State University, offers a valuable commentary on conceptual issues underlying learning. Her book, *Psychology of Learning for Instruction,* applies learning theories to the practical issues involved in effective instructional design. She considers learning and defines it as:

> A persisting change in performance or performance potential that results from experience or interaction with the world. A learning theory, then, is a set of constructs linking observed changes in performance with what is thought to bring about those changes. Instruction is about the deliberate arrangement of learning conditions to promote the attaining of some intended goal; an instructional theory can provide principles by which teachers and instructional designers can assure learning.[3]

The theoretical analysis can be extended by distinguishing between two major frameworks:

♦ One framework considers how content and knowledge is *transmitted* for the learner.
♦ A second framework considers how the learner *transforms* information, generates hypotheses, and makes decisions about the content and knowledge.

At a crude level, the former can be characterized as an instructor-centered approach and the latter as a learner-centered approach. Neither framework should be regarded as preferable. Those responsible for training must consider all aspects of effective design. In Proposition 6, it was argued that the distinction between learning and training is of value and should be maintained. Using this distinction, the first framework can be regarded as a training framework and the second as a learning framework.

Zane Berge, a writer in the field of learning technology, developed a most effective analysis of the value of an approach that considers frameworks. The discussion that follows is drawn from his analysis.[4]

One of the key concepts in a *transmission* framework is that a teacher can pass on a fixed body of information; the student or learner interacts with prepackaged content. The skill of the teacher lies in the selection of the content and in teaching style to produce a specific outcome from the students.

Transformation frameworks necessarily emphasize individual thinking and construction of meaning. Training under this approach is more tentative, flexible, and experimental; hence, it is student or learner centered. In this context, a community of learners will improve learning through their interaction.

Berge is interested in the practical issues involved in developing an effective model for distance education and training in the organization:

> The biggest differences in various models of distance education center around the assumptions underlying the educational philosophy of the model builder. Some models are designed for industrialized or prepackaged knowledge . . . others are more flexible, customized to the individual and organic . . .
>
> While there are many variations of distance training mainly differing by the types of technology used . . . basically the difference rests in the control aspect. In some models, the trainer and the organization have primary control, and in others control resides with the trainee. . . . A second dimension involves whether or not the model used involves distributing instruction to groups of participants at a given place or is designed for individual participation with some type of asynchronous communication medium being used.[5]

The term *synchronous* (and its antonym *asynchronous*) is used frequently in discussions on distance learning. A definition is offered in Focus Point 17.

> ### *Focus Point 17: Synchronous and Asynchronous Learning*
>
> The distinction is simple:
>
> > Sychronous learning is real-time learning that takes place when all participants are involved at the same time. Recipients of synchronous learning need not be in the same place: Two-way video, for example, is synchronous and allows interaction between student and teacher.
> >
> > Asynchronous learning occurs when content is built at one time but accessed at another. It is "time shifted" and can allow learners access at their own convenience. Common content can be prepared and delivered when needed (possibly just in time).
>
> These are my own distinctions to emphasize the difference from the training manager's perspective. A more precise definition embedded in the technology of distance learning and education is available in Berge's *Distance Training*.[6]

Some readers may regard this discussion as too theoretical. It is worth remembering, however, that the discipline of ISD is underpinned by a solid theoretical base. That base takes into account both transmission and transformation frameworks. The result is an emphasis on the design of effective instructional material. It would be a tragedy if, in the rush to implement e-learning, an inappropriate product was produced and delivered because basic distinctions were lost. Both Berge's and Driscoll's works are well worth reading if this danger is to be avoided.

On a lighter note, another insight to be gained from reading Berge's *Distance Training* is his introduction of David Thornburg's engaging categorization of venues for learning. These are set out in Focus Point 18.

How can the information gained from the campfire and watering hole be captured and shared?

Thornburg's primordial metaphors should be helpful whenever e-learning is implemented. What are the possibilities and problems

> ### Focus Point 18: Venues for Learning
>
> David Thornburg introduces the idea of three venues for learning, drawn from primordial metaphors[7]:
>
> ♦ *Campfires:* For thousands of years storytelling around the campfire has been used as an occasion when people sit at the foot of the elders and become informed. This sharing of knowledge, skills, and wisdom continues to be a critical element in teaching and learning.
>
> ♦ *The watering hole:* This is different in that, historically, people shared information with neighbors who just happened to be there. It is more informal and haphazard, with stimulating exchanges and gossips. The essence is a shared culture and social learning.
>
> ♦ *The cave:* This is a secluded personal space where a person can take what has been learned from others and make sense of it. Knowledge or insights are internalized or made one's own in this space.
>
> One other useful metaphor is suggested by Thornburg's classification:
>
> ♦ *The hunting expedition:* Here, a group of individuals embark on a task together and their skills and capabilities are exposed to the outside world. Individuals can learn from each other, a process that is particularly effective if the more experienced are aware of their need to assist the less experienced.

in delivering content to the cave and in facilitating learning on the hunting expedition? How can the information gained from the campfire and watering hole be captured and shared? These issues are central to learner support. Readers may wish to reflect on their own preferred venue for learning. Mine is a cave in Norfolk, England, where I read, reflect, and write while my wife travels to the nearest market town to hunt mammoth for dinner.

Learning Preferences and Styles

There is an evident link here with individual learning preferences. People learn in different ways, and one of the skills of successful teaching is to adapt the approach to the individual. Peter Honey and Alan Mumford have developed and popularized a most successful model in the United Kingdom. It draws, in part, from the work of David Kolb, an American academic and consultant.[8]

Kolb introduced the concept of the learning cycle: At stage one a person starts off with an experience; at stage two he or she observes and reflects on that experience; at stage three, he or she develops certain principles and concepts from that reflection; and at stage four, he or she tests these principles and concepts either by replicating the initial experience or by trying out the principles in new circumstances. This will produce a new experience (stage one again) and the cycle continues. Some advocates of this approach suggest that the individual's experience of the learning cycle could be paralleled in the organization. In this case, it is particularly important that the organization ensure that there is adequate opportunity for stages two and three of the cycle (respectively called systematic reflection and abstract conceptualization) to take place.

Honey and Mumford's contribution was to postulate how a learning cycle could be used to identify individual learning styles. For them all the evidence suggested that individuals have learning styles. In the early 1980s, they published a manual of learning styles that included a most useful and practical questionnaire; it was updated and reissued in 2000.[9]

Honey offers the following seven assertions about learning:

1. Learning is both a process and an outcome. We use the same word to describe both aspects. Some confusion can arise and we are generally much more comfortable talking about the outcome than concentrating on the process.
2. Learning is not just about knowledge. It is also about skills, insights, beliefs, values, attitudes, habits, feelings, wisdom, shared understanding, and self-awareness. In other words, it covers a multitude of things.
3. Learning outcomes can be desirable or undesirable for the learner and for others.
4. Learning processes can be conscious or unconscious. People can

learn when they do not realize that they are learning and certainly can learn as an incidental result of other activity.

5. Conscious learning processes can be proactive or reactive. A lot of learning can be reflective after the event, but we can set ourselves goals or objectives that will assist.

6. The learning process occurs inside the individual, but making the outcomes explicit, as well as sharing them with others, adds value to the learning.

7. There is no one right way to learn for everybody and for every situation.

The last of these assertions brings us to the heart of Honey and Mumford's contribution: Learning style is about preference. Honey's favored term is *learning style preferences*.

Honey and Mumford's approach is illustrated in Figure 5-2. The lowercase letters describe the learning cycle. Learners may start from any one of the four elements. Each element contributes to an interac-

FIGURE 5-2
The learning cycle.

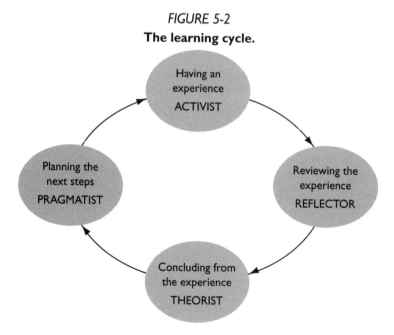

(Reproduced with permission of Peter Honey Learning.)

tive learning process. The uppercase letters are descriptions of four learning style preferences associated in turn with each element of the cycle. In summary:

♦ *Activists* like to take direct action, are enthusiastic, and welcome new challenges and experiences. They are primarily interested in the here and now and less interested in putting things into a broader context.

♦ *Reflectors* like to think about things in detail before taking action. They take a thoughtful approach and are good listeners. They will welcome the opportunity to repeat a piece of learning.

♦ *Theorists* like to see how things fit into a pattern. They are logical, objective, systems people who prefer a sequential approach to problems, are analytical, pay great attention to detail, and tend to be perfectionists.

♦ *Pragmatists* like to see how things work in practice and enjoy experimenting with new ideas. They are practical, down to earth, and like solving problems. They appreciate the opportunity to try out what they have learned.

This is a rich and helpful analysis with evident practical implications for learners and trainers.

Learners who are aware of their preferences can select learning opportunities that match their style preferences. They can seek (and be assisted) to become balanced learners by strengthening underutilized preferences. Trainers, as enablers of learning, can make the whole learning process explicit and can use learning style preferences to encourage group learning activity.

The central questions for the training professional remain unchanged.

The platform for the delivery of training changes with the arrival of the Internet. However, the central questions for the training professional remain unchanged: How do people learn best and how can we help people to learn more effectively? An appreciation of the theoretical frameworks provides a helpful background from which to work.

This consideration of learning styles offers one useful area of insight. Other issues concern motivation (which is considered next) and, to reflect on Thornburg's categorization set out in Focus Point 18, time and space to learn. All can be brought together in Proposition 15.

Proposition 15

There will be a renewed interest in learner motivation, learning preferences and styles, and time and space to learn.

Motivation to Learn

That high motivation on the part of the student is an important enabler for learning can be readily accepted. To illustrate, at Ernst & Young there are three occasions when employees display a singular thirst for knowledge:

♦ When they have just joined the organization and are eager to gain the background information needed to make a contribution and gain the respect and confidence of their colleagues
♦ When they are nearing the time of professional examinations that will give them valued qualifications
♦ When they are approaching partner admission and need to satisfy the requirements of a demanding assessment center

Nothing else quite captures the energy employees display at these points in their career. They are motivated by the fact that there will be clear paybacks for positive results.

Alas, not all learning events have such an immediate payback, but plenty of information and guidance are available to suggest ways of improving motivation. Learner motivation is something that the training manager can influence. Earlier we discussed Marcy Driscoll's work on learning theory. In her book, *Psychology of Learning for Instruction,* she offers the following analysis of the main sources of motivation to learn:[10]

♦ Curiosity and interest
♦ Goals and goal orientation

♦ Self-efficacy beliefs (the ability to organize and execute the causes of action required to produce given attainments)

These factors all relate to the individual's motivation to learn before the learning has actually begun and during a learning event. Other factors concern the learner's continued desire to study or participate. This aspect is about the skills required to monitor progress and achieve self-regulation.

Stimulating motivation through effective instructional strategy is the subject of many texts. In addition to Driscoll's book, Professor Raymond J. Wlodkowski's *Enhancing Adult Motivation to Learn* is highly recommended.[11]

It should not be forgotten that one way of improving learner motivation is to identify and remove barriers to learning. There are many reasons that individuals might prefer not to learn. Some will be specific to the situation in the organization, but a general list would include the following:[12]

♦ The fear of demonstrating a lack of skill or competence
♦ A general lack of awareness of the need to develop or of the opportunities available
♦ The need to blame others for inadequate performance or capability rather than taking responsibility for one's own actions or feelings
♦ A lack of personal confidence
♦ A general belief that people cannot change

Time and Space to Learn

The third element of Proposition 15 concerns individual preferences: When and where do people learn best? Considering how important this is to the future of e-learning, there is a paucity of general research information on the subject, let alone information specific to an organization.

For example, in the early 1990s, the CD-ROM emerged as the preferred tool for technology-based training. There was a movement to establish learning centers that would contain libraries of CD-ROMs and other distance-learning materials. Vendors of multimedia training tools gave added momentum to the movement by offering special discounts on training materials or, in some cases, an outsourced management arrangement.

Two case studies at the end of this chapter demonstrate that there is much to be said for dedicated facilities where staff can access learning materials. Both Motorola, in developing its learning strategy at its corporate university, and British Airways, in reassessing its QUEST and communication points, are reviewing the place of learning centers. They have adopted different but considered approaches.

Generally, there is an embarrassing lack of published information on the use and acceptability of learning resource centers. Inquirers are left with a distinct feeling that they may not have been successful, appealing only to a minority of potential users and contributing little to organizational objectives. Many may have been quietly forgotten. Training managers are good at burying their dead ideas; however, they are not as good at organizing (still less, publicizing) the memorial service. Recent research has been undertaken by the MASIE Center and by the ASTD on time and space in learning. In May 2000, Elliott Masie of the MASIE Center, whose wider contribution was introduced in Chapter 2, published the results of a short survey entitled "Learning at Our Busy Desks."[13] The survey was delivered electronically, and the sample was drawn from the 3,000 respondents who receive his regular e-mailed newsletter. Despite limitations of the sample population, the survey does offer some useful results, which are summarized in Focus Point 19.

The clear preference indicated from this survey is to work at the desk on the organization's time. This obviously raises some problems in ensuring the necessary privacy. Some manufacturers of office furniture are addressing the issue by designing furniture that allows screens or pods to be put in place.

Commenting on the survey's results, Masie has introduced the concept of organizational surround. His argument is that course-based training invariably begins with a "drum roll." Participants arrive; the door is closed; they write their names on a badge or name tent. This is generally followed by introductions and an opening ritual (a favor-

2,474
responses

Focus Point 19: Learning at Our Desks:
A Summary of Survey Results

If you were about to participate in an important learning activity, where would you want to do it?

Results:	at my desk	47 percent
	in a conference room/learning center	
	at work	30 percent
	at home	21 percent
	on the road	1 percent
	on a bus or a train whilst commuting	1 percent

If you were to take this class at your desk, when would you most likely take it?

Results:	during work	49 percent
	before work	16 percent
	after work	17 percent
	at lunch	16 percent
	on my days off	2 percent

Results from those people who had an office with a door, or work as a trainer, indicated a more positive response to working at the desk.

(Reproduced with permission and thanks to the Masie Center.)

ite is to ask participants whether they are volunteers, skeptics, or hostages at the course; this is commended as a way of teasing out the dissidents). The instructor then proceeds.

If e-learning is to be effective, it must take place in an appropriate organizational surround.

This "drum roll" signals a change in atmosphere. Participants are there to learn—even in the age of mobile technology, concentration can be guaranteed for the first ten minutes. Other staff members are expected to respect the fact that the course member is off-site and unavailable.

E-learning, however, does not begin with an introductory drum roll. There are no shared rituals; there is no change in atmosphere. Masie argues powerfully that if e-learning is to be effective, it must take place in an appropriate organizational surround—this must involve physical signals to colleagues that learning is taking place. One obvious way of achieving this goal is to create special learning spaces or centers. Masie's view is that unless the learning center is within close proximity and is available for ninety-minute sessions without prior reservation, it is unlikely to offer an acceptable alternative to learning at the desk.

Learner Acceptability: The IBM Research

There is a greater need for information, both generally and specific to the training manager's organization, in all aspects of learning. A useful study undertaken by IBM Management Development, reported on in the ASTD's journal, *Training and Development,* offers insights into the acceptability of e-learning technology.[14] In this article, Nancy Lewis and Peter Orton argue that, at present, many people do not understand enough about e-learning to be able to assess their preferences.

An exercise was undertaken at IBM using a technique known as conjoint analysis. Essentially this examines trade-offs to determine which combination of attributes is most satisfying to the customer. Conjoint analysis is a well-established consumer survey technique when the attributes are well-understood; for example, house price against number of bedrooms. However, the exercise could not produce robust results:

> Knowledge learning preferences can inform instructional designs, but only if learners understand all of the variables and features. The current problem with learning interventions is that not all choices are salient to learners and, especially with online learning, not all attributes are understood.[15]

So far, encounters have been mixed:

> In fact, many users' experiences with online learning have been fraught with long download waits, choppy video, confusing navigation, and endless text screens. For some people, just having to install a plug-in can roadblock any sampling of online instruction. Many, if not all, learners have scant knowledge of what a dynamic engaging online experience can be.[16]

IBM Management Development was faced with the problem of rolling out a new learning intervention, Basic Blue for Managers. This intervention involved fifty weeks devoted to e-learning. IBM commissioned Professor Youngme Moon of Harvard Business School to assess general preferences for different approaches to delivering learning. A random sample of sixty-three new IBM managers was surveyed by questionnaire. Despite their high level of technology awareness, new IBM managers reported a preference for classroom learning over online learning (the term used in the survey).

However, when Professor Moon conducted postprogram interviews, she found that respondents commended both approaches to learning—classroom and online—with equal enthusiasm. Moreover,

> Most telling was that all respondents answered that they preferred learning the informational material (the cognitive-based development) online from their home or office rather than in a classroom setting.

> Conversely, the managers preferred learning the behavioral-skills material in a classroom environment rather than in an online setting.[17]

Professor Moon concluded that after they had experienced online learning, respondents indicated that they preferred an approach that was best suited to content. Key factors were the amount and type of material presented and the time available to review it: "The key was the hybrid model. Rather than adopting a totally online program, they decided to take a best-of-both-worlds approach, and it really worked."[18]

Learner Acceptability: Will They Come?

Many of the issues that we have discussed were considered in a research study undertaken by the ASTD and the MASIE Center.[19]

Jointly they undertook a survey of e-learning in practice of thirty courses at sixteen companies in the United States; feedback was obtained from more than 700 learners. The aim was to analyze the relationship between the organization's efforts to market and motivate learner participation and the satisfaction of the end user—the learner. It is encouraging to see such objective and "vendor-neutral" research taking place: The greater the focus on the learner and the more objectivity, the better. The results were published in June 2001 as *E-Learning: If We Build It, Will They Come?*

The study concentrated on three particular features of the content in which e-learning is delivered: marketing of the initiatives, support for the learners, and the effect of incentives on the individual learner's willingness to participate. The survey, however, restricted itself to the willingness of individual learners to start courses. It did not collect findings on the factors that influence the learner's willingness to complete courses, an increasingly important issue.

The findings were varied but one of the most significant was the importance of effective support:

> Although **marketing and promotion** efforts appeared to be the crucial factor in prompting learners to begin the courses in the study, they were not always likely to engage in the portions of these courses delivered via technology. Rather it was the amount of **support** learners received that actually increased their willingness to begin the technology delivered portions. The level to which learners felt they were supported was one of the primary indicators regarding their participation in e-learning.[20]

The study particularly emphasizes the need for manager and co-worker support in providing learners with sufficient time to take the course and in offering encouragement to complete it. The seasoned training manager may react to this with a sigh of "I've been there a hundred times before." The need for commitment and support from the training manager has been emphasized again and again. An important new perspective is emerging here. E-learning will not work as an activity where the learner proceeds in isolation. As the study indicates, the manager should:

◆ Explain why the learner should take the course.

♦ Point out the connections between the course, the workplace, and the individual's career.

♦ Give status to the course in the same way as status is given to classroom training.

♦ Provide a context and opportunities to transfer to the workplace.

Additionally, peer or coworker support can help by providing a dialogue and assist with these transfer opportunities.

All this emphasizes that e-learning is not a quick fix to be undertaken simply to save costs. This conclusion is stressed by another feature of the study—that learner satisfaction is greatly influenced by the learner's previous experiences with e-learning. Learners who reported having previously had negative experiences with e-learning were significantly less satisfied with their current e-learning experience than those who had not previously had negative experiences. This finding underscores the importance of the learner's initial experience with e-learning.[21]

One other set of findings, although perhaps more intuitively obvious, concerns the location and timing of events. Learners who took courses on the road or at a client's premises were less satisfied with the experience than those who did not. Additionally, there was an overwhelming preference to take e-learning during working hours; learners do not want technology to disrupt their personal life.

The overall conclusion must be that "organizations cannot rely on the technology itself to drive interest, acceptance or satisfaction with e-learning. . . . While companies can indeed view e-learning as an efficient new means for educating employees, the context in which the learning is offered must be carefully managed."[22]

We have been warned!

Learner Acceptability: The Global Dimension

This paucity of hard accessible information from research is even more evident when the international implications of e-learning are considered. What problems will be encountered when material is used outside the country where it is produced? Are difficulties of cultural acceptability likely to be encountered? How generic is material—will it travel?

How will an interviewing skills module produced in the United States be received in India or Finland or China or Cuba? Business strategy or technical computer skills may be standard but the softer skills such as feedback, listening, and assertiveness must surely be grounded in social mores and cultures.

The critical questions for all trainers who are likely to be involved in global e-learning projects are as follows: If learning content (for example, lectures, presentations, questionnaires, video clips) is produced elsewhere in the world, how acceptable would it be in your country and organization? If learning content produced internationally is distributed to learners in your country, what sort of learner support would be required and who would deliver it?

It would be a brave training manager who would say that he or she could answer these questions with confidence now. We are all on a learning curve and need better research information. We must also be prepared to share our thoughts, ideas, and experiences.

One possible route for developing some answers could be to examine some of the models of global culture and speculate on what they could tell us about the acceptance of e-learning. At the 2001 ASTD conference, this problem of cultural differences was put to one of the leading experts on e-learning, Sivasailam "Thiagi" Thiagarajan, who has a wealth of practical international experience.[23] His answer began: "There are cultural differences; we have a lot of data on cultural differences; we need to know what differences make a difference in the acceptance/use of e-learning; we do not yet have enough data on this topic."

He suggested that, when designing e-learning, the program should be made as lean as possible if it is going to be used in different cultures. Special care must be taken with examples and illustrations. Where possible, there should be a facility to develop any additions locally, so that they can find cultural acceptance.

Such sentiments will be echoed by many training professionals who are currently wrestling with the challenge of implementing e-learning systems in global organizations. The Ernst & Young Learning Connection offers a good example and forms the final case study of this chapter.

Learning in the New Context

It is now appropriate to weave together the strands of this chapter. For the training profession, the overall picture is depressing. We simply do not know what we need to know.

We simply do not know what we need to know.

Few would disagree with the central argument and propositions we have discussed. The new technology offers the trainer the opportunity to deliver interventions to suit the learner's needs. This will result in the emergence of a new discipline of learner support. Knowledge about how people learn is essential for effective interventions. Information on motivation, learning preferences and styles, and preferences of time and space need to be carefully considered.

Useful work has undoubtedly been undertaken on updating the instructional development framework—and there is extensive theoretical literature available on learning and training. The individuals and organizations cited in this chapter have all offered useful insights.

However, the stark truth is that e-learning takes place in a radically changed context from the classroom model. Although the questions to be asked may be the same, the answers could be quite different. Much of the research base is inappropriate. For example, academic research often uses students for the "sample participants." Furthermore, much of the data offered by vendors of products are specific to those products, and they are unlikely to wish to publicize failure.

Focus Point 20 lists some simple questions that are central to learner support in any organization. For those of us who are training manag-

Focus Point 20: The Key Questions to Learner Support

For each individual learner:

♦ How do they prefer to learn?
  —What is their learning style preference and what is the impact of e-learning on this style?
♦ When do they prefer to learn?
  —Do they prefer to learn in small bites or at an extended session?
♦ Where do they prefer to learn?
  —Do they prefer to learn at their desk, in specific rooms or spaces at the office, or at home?

ers, this is what we need to know: the how, when, and where preferences of learners in our organizations. The hope is that we can develop methodologies and share information.

In that spirit, an Ernst & Young questionnaire is included in Focus Point 21. It was designed to determine user reaction to a new learning portal and offered individuals the chance to see what learning opportunities were available and to prepare a personal learning plan based on that information. Readers are welcome to adapt the questionnaire to their own needs.

Notes

1 My thanks to my colleague at Ernst & Young, Brenton Hague, who introduced me to the approach outlined in Figure 5-1.

2 I am grateful to Dr. Michael Molenda, associate professor, Instructional Systems Technology, University of Indiana, for introducing me to this term and for his advice on its application. Like Daniel, Molenda uses the term to refer to intellectual techniques and processes, although he focuses more on processes related to instruction, such as instructional design. He also uses the term *soft technologies of instruction* to refer to specific formats or templates that have been developed to hold various types of subject context.

(*Notes continued on page 128.*)

Focus Point 21: Ernst & Young Questionnaire

Name   Office/Location

Department   Grade

L&D Manager

1 General reaction

How would you rate the potential overall value/usefulness of the portal?

No value   Very valuable

| 1 | 2 | 3 | 4 | 5 | 6 | 7 | 8 | 9 | 10 |

What could be done to improve its potential value/usefulness?

---

2 General ease of use

Did you find it easy to navigate?

Very difficult   Very easy

| 1 | 2 | 3 | 4 | 5 | 6 | 7 | 8 | 9 | 10 |

Please provide examples of areas that were difficult to use:

Did you encounter any technology-related difficulties when using the portal?
For example, access, transferring information, speed of response.

None   Significant issues encountered

| 1 | 2 | 3 | 4 | 5 | 6 | 7 | 8 | 9 | 10 |

Please provide details below

Did you seek support to help you with any difficulties encountered?

Never   Frequently

I   2   3   4   5   6   7   8   9   10

Please provide examples of what support you needed and who you contacted:

3 Cultural feedback

How easy was it to find time to use the portal?

Did you primarily work in the office or at home when using the portal? Please provide a summary of when and where you used the portal.

4 Application

Did you construct a Personal Learning Plan? YES/NO

Please comment on your plan below. For example, how many different courses were included?

What did you do with your plan after its completion? Did you discuss it with your counseling manager/colleagues/L&D manager?

5 Future of the portal

What additional information/functionality would you like to see on the portal which could assist you in planning your learning?

6 Other comments

Please add other comments which you think would assist.

3   M. P. Driscoll, *Psychology of Learning for Instruction,* 2nd ed. (Needham Heights, Mass.: Allyn & Bacon, 2000).

4   Z. L. Berge, "Conceptual Frameworks in Distance Training and Education," in *Distance Training,* ed. Z. L. Berge and D. A. Schreiber (San Francisco: Jossey-Bass, 1998), 19–36.

5   Ibid., 24.

6   Ibid., 411–18.

7   D. D. Thornburg, "Campfires in Cyberspace: Primordial Metaphors for Learning in the 21st Century," *www.tcpd.org/thornburg/handouts/Campfires.pdf.*

8   D. Kolb, *Experiental Learning* (Englewood Cliffs, N.J.: Prentice-Hall, 1984).

9   P. Honey and A. Mumford, *The Learning Styles Questionnaire (80-item version)* (Maidenhead, U.K.: Peter Honey Publications, 2000).

10 Driscoll, 306ff.

11 R. J. Wlodkowski, *Enhancing Adult Motivation to Learn,* rev. ed. (San Francisco: Jossey-Bass, 1999).

12 My thanks to Karen Jaques of Dove Nest for suggesting this aspect of improving motivation.

13 E. Masie, "Learning at Our Busy Desks," *Learning Decisions,* May 2000, 1–2, 4–5.

14 N. J. Lewis and P. Orton, "The Five Attributes of Innovative E-Learning," *Training and Development,* June 2000, 47–51.

15 Ibid., 47.

16 Ibid., 48.

17 Ibid.

18 Ibid., 49.

19 ASTD/The MASIE Center, *E-Learning: If We Build It, Will They Come?* (Alexandria, Va.: ASTD, 2001). Page references in notes 21–23 refer to the executive summary document.

20 Ibid., 4.

21 Ibid., 6.

22 Ibid., 7.

23 I am most grateful to Sivasailam "Thiagi" Thiagarajan for his insights on this problem (*www.thiagi.com*).

LEARNING AT MOTOROLA UNIVERSITY, EMEA

Motorola is a leading global company providing integrated communications solutions and embedded electronic solutions to its customers. It employs 140,000 people worldwide. Motorola University (MU) was initially launched in the 1970s as the Motorola

Training and Education Center. Since then, it has attracted much attention, reflecting the growing interest in corporate universities.

This case concerns one aspect of MU's training activity: its approach to the implementation of technology-enabled learning for its staff of 23,000 in Europe, the Middle East, and Africa (EMEA). Motorola's intention is to make 30 percent of training available by alternative (nonclassroom) means by 2001, rising to 50 percent by 2003. This presents a considerable challenge for the MU EMEA staff. Content, delivery channels, and support for learners all must be considered if the transfer away from classroom-based training is to be effective. Moreover, this transfer must take place in a global context; the key educational alliances with the university providers are determined in the United States. Extending technology-enabled learning throughout the world (with access for all employees) is considered critical to the company's business success. MU's motto is "Right knowledge, right now."

In the words of Dr. John O'Connor, EMEA education technology integrator:

> People in the telecommunications business need knowledge on several levels, including technical know-how, product-specific knowledge and competitive intelligence. Each of these requires a dynamic and evolving educational framework. The classroom model cannot efficiently deliver for large, disparate population groups. Motorolans need information that is relevant, up to date, on time and in manageable chunks. Learning technologies can play a strong part in making this scenario successful.

Production and Delivery of Content
The targeted 30 percent of training to be made available by nonclassroom means embraces several technology-based approaches. It may include, for example, a synchronous satellite course broadcast from the United States. Many self-study courses are offered through both intranet (Web) access and CD-ROM format. The materials are both generic (vendor supplied) and internally customized to Motorola's needs as necessary. Sub-

jects range from management and interpersonal skills to engineering.

Two innovations in learning technology are currently at an advanced stage. The first is an approach called Intranet Immediate Instruction (or I-cubed/I³). This is a hardware/software solution that streams video images with audio, allowing subject matter experts within Motorola to produce one-off and regular messages or teaching modules. I-cubed is deployed within Motorola using a combination of tools that include Microsoft's MediaPlayer viewer application. The education technology specialists have prepared both design and presenter guidelines to ensure that the final product is built on solid learning principles. MU has demonstrated that with well-designed storyboards and scripts, internal customers (worldwide) can access relevant, engaging messages or learning modules on the company intranet within fifteen minutes of creation.

It is apparent that this type of solution spans communications as well as training—yet another illustration of the information age phenomenon referred to as "blur." In the first three months of I-cubed's operation, a series of diverse training modules were developed and distributed. Topics include wireless access protocol technology, product technical updates, performance review procedures, and new employee induction.

The second innovation is the creation of a virtual reality (VR) PC-based solution laboratory for factory workers, which was designed to increase operational efficiency through off-line training. Using a matrix of digitized photographs and video and text/audio script within a VR modeling framework, the operation of an assembly machine can be simulated in all its operations. The intention is to make this training available adjacent to the production line in designated Motorola factories.

Learner Support and Learning Centers
The nature of the business and its culture means that the company must expect Motorolans (their preferred term) to become receptive to technology-enabled learning. Most employees have

PCs, and for those who do not, or when geographical constraints inhibit access to the intranet, the training can always be supplied on a CD-ROM. MU works with local learning representatives in many locations to assist with access or other problems.

In addition, MU has established learning centers at eight locations across the EMEA region. A typical learning center has networked PCs with an administrator available to offer support. Other learning resources available at these facilities include books, videos, tapes, periodicals, and language courses. Learning centers offer learning privacy in a supportive environment where people can become comfortable with PC-based learning. O'Connor states: "Learning centers may be thought of as a bridge between where we are in self-directed learning and where we'd like to be. If we were to build new learning areas, they might take the form of smaller kiosks nearer the workplace."

In O'Connor's view, learning centers have historically focused on creating a broad resource library at the expense of the specific needs of learners. In some cases, learning centers have been established without a strong business case (or indeed any business case at all). Realistically, these facilities need to be interwoven with the site-based business and performance needs to ensure that they do not evolve into wasteful or redundant "landmarks." Assuming that the business need exists, constant marketing then becomes a key part of the success formula.

Motorola has been regarded as an early adopter of learning technology and is confident of its future. E-learning will grow in importance as pressures on time intensify. O'Connor notes: "Many people will look for five-minute learning interventions."

However, MU is realistic about the limitations of technology-based approaches and the need to facilitate their acceptance. A recent Finance for Managers training program was designed to include a combination of CD-ROM training with "live" coaching elements. Some users were confident with just content, whereas others needed more face-to-face support from a finance "coach," indicating different requirements for structure and social interaction with other learners. In O'Connor's words, "Go to the Web for definitions—go to the classroom for practice."

The way of the future, then, is a balance among different forms of learning media. However, with technology-based methods increasing as a proportion of the total, more responsibility is placed on learners to plan, conduct, and evaluate their own learning. O'Connor describes the immediate e-learning future as "self-directed within a disciplined framework." More stringent milestones and a clearer support structure will need to be embedded if the full gains from new technology are to be realized.

Author's Note: My thanks to Dr. O'Connor and Motorola University EMEA for their assistance in the preparation of this case study.

BRITISH AIRWAYS QUEST AND COMMUNICATION POINTS

For some time, training professionals working for British Airways have been considering the issues involved in time and space to learn. They were offered a unique opportunity to implement a purpose design-solution when the company opened a new headquarters. The experience is outlined herein. British Airways does not claim to have solved the issues involved in time and space to learn and is currently reorienting and redesigning its approach. It is therefore particularly helpful that British Airways has agreed to share its experience.

Background

In 1997, British Airways moved its corporate headquarters to a new building, Waterside. Some 2,500 employees would be located at this new purpose-built site. All would need access to training and to be able to participate in other communication activities built on new technologies.

Accordingly, in advance of the move, a series of technology trials was conducted. The trials examined how well training was received through the following delivery platforms: a discrete designated workstation in an office area, individual desktops using CD-ROMs, and individual desktops via the local area network. The trials were designed to simulate full multimedia to the desktop in a low-technology environment. This allowed the identification and preparation of a plan for the most appropriate method of delivery given the access to high-bandwidth technology in the new building.

The report produced at the end of these trials stated:

> The preferred option for delivery is for a discrete workstation. Trialists reported that they were interrupted regularly when sitting at their own desk, as they were seen as accessible by colleagues. Telephones and e-mail were also a distraction to learning. The discrete area option was the preferred option for all the trialists, providing a more local learning environment considered better than the desk.

This "discrete area option" had applications beyond training. There was a need to deliver other technology-led activities that could best be described as communications. Particularly important were those that used video, including desktop video conferencing, stored videos, and British Airways TV (a service designed to give staff information on current matters as they affect the business).

The chosen solution was to establish "QUEST and Communication Points." QUEST (an established internal brand) signaled that learning opportunities were available; communication emphasized the other technologies.

Forty-five separate QUEST and communication points were installed at chosen locations in the Waterside building. Each contained a high-specification PC that was branded to distinguish it from other desktop PCs. All could be used for applications by one or two people at the same time, all were connected to a fast transmission network, and all were screened to ensure privacy.

Formally, the QUEST and communication points and network were corporately funded by the information management department. Because of copyright and licensing restrictions, the programs were mainly limited to internally produced courses, although a number of licensed IT training modules were available.

Although the initiative produced some positive results, it was recognized that there was a need to increase the effectiveness and impact. In March 1999, a review showed that training was the most accessed resource at the QUEST and communication points. The usage statistics highlighted the fact that the points were most used in the areas that had promoted their use and had requested additional coaching. Julia Hilger-Ellis of the British Airways training team summed up the situation in the following terms: "We will use the knowledge gained from the trials and implementation of the points to shape our future e-learning strategy."

Generally, the following difficulties were identified. First, the QUEST and communication points were not always in the right locations. Second, there had been insufficient marketing. Third, the support required by some learners had not always been available at the time that it was required. Fourth, ownership and responsibility for the initiative was not sufficiently clear. Finally, there had been uncertainty on purpose: The points had been introduced at the same time as several other changes following relocation to Waterside.

Currently, British Airways is relaunching the initiative, which will now be firmly owned by the training function. There will be a new marketing campaign, preceded by a consultation about location. In addition, a greater range of e-learning options will be made available through this platform. QUEST and communication points will, however, remain part of British Airways strategy.

Author's Note: My thanks to Julia Hilger-Ellis and the British Airways training team for their assistance in the preparation of this case study.

THE ERNST & YOUNG LEARNING CONNECTION

The Ernst & Young Learning Connection (EYLC) is the term used to describe Ernst & Young's global e-learning initiative. The firm has decided to rebrand the LEAP technology (Learning Environment to Accelerate Performance) offered by Intellinex to align the learning offering with its People First Strategy, connecting and developing its employees for competitive advantage. The history and development of Ernst & Young's e-learning system, and the establishment of Intellinex as an e-learning venture, were described in the first case study included at the end of Chapter 2. Given the successful establishment of an e-learning system, there are powerful arguments for using EYLC as a global learning platform with potential access for all the firm's 78,000 employees in 131 countries.

The decision was firmly business based; global learning is seen as a direct response to global client expectations. Many of Ernst & Young's clients operate throughout the world. They include Coca-Cola, Ford, United Bank of Switzerland, BP, Compaq, British Airways, and America Online. Global clients expect that their business advisers operate on this basis and that their methodologies and processes be consistent in different countries. Those responsible for training are therefore faced with a stark choice: Either people are moved around the world (at a prohibitive cost) or technology enablers are utilized.

The business argument is well illustrated within the United Kingdom, where one of the key drivers for implementation was the ability to deliver consistent learning using the firm's global process. Another was related to the management of client relations (sales and account methodologies).

From the learner's viewpoint, there are also benefits for the corporate argument. These were considered in an internal paper delivered to the *Ernst & Young Global Executive* in September 2001 and are as follows:

- Having 24-hour, 7-day access
- Stepping up to changes quickly
- Building technical skills and knowledge rapidly
- Having technologically enabled links to personal development plans
- Acquiring personal and business skills

The first step toward a commitment to the global adoption of the Intellinex systems and technology within Ernst & Young took place in Stuttgart, Germany, in April 2000. Representatives from ten of the largest country practices (senior business leaders as well as HR and training specialists) spent several days investigating alternatives. They emerged with an articulated global learning strategy; an agreed-upon common structure around learning; a commitment to common technology; and, to some extent, an acceptable global content. In March 2001, the *Ernst & Young Global Executive* approved a global learning connection that was adopted to describe the global rollout of e-learning.

At that time, the Intellinex approach and LEAP technology were well implemented in the United States (see the case study at the end of Chapter 2 for further details). The United Kingdom, as the second largest practice, was chosen as the first country for release of the new global product. The launch in the United Kingdom took place in October 2001 with nine other countries, including the United States, adopting the new system with a view to completion by July 2002.

There are also evident advantages for participant countries. They will get access to a common content pool. This will comprise about 500 hours of internally generated Ernst & Young learning material on assurance/audit, tax, and corporate finance. Over time the plan is to add several times as much material purchased or licensed from content providers covering generic areas such as IT and soft-skills management techniques. Ernst & Young plans to author Web-based learning that is custom-made using appropriate Intellinex tools. This material will be hosted on an ASP in the United States and delivered to the desktop via the Internet.

Implementation in the United Kingdom

The U.K. practice delivers about half a million hours of training to its 8,200 employees; many different learning options are involved. In the first year that the EYLC is launched, about half a day's training (5 percent) will be delivered using e-learning solutions. This is expected, over time, to rise to 30–40 percent.

Finola Harrington, learning and development operations director at Ernst & Young, commented that the key criteria for transition to e-learning were as follows:

♦ Is there a high level of interest in the topic area and therefore high volume?
♦ Is the topic area stable? (two-year shelf life)
♦ Is it an area where consistency and efficiencies can be achieved quickly?

In the first year, the U.K. firm will spend about £750,000 in establishing the e-learning system. This will involve creation of the Web site, establishment of the assured systems, and five person-years of project team time. The intention is to make the first year "cost neutral"—compensating cuts in course-based training will take place. After the first year, the aim is progressively to cut costs and increase savings by 15 percent per year over the following three-year period. This is a more impressive figure than might appear, because new learning opportunities are emerging all the time.

Implementation in Germany

Dr. Sylvia Broening is responsible for the strategic development and implementation of e-learning in Germany. There are 3,000 Ernst & Young employees spread across five major locations in the country, with the largest office in Stuttgart. The vast majority are auditors or tax specialists. Some modest e-learning took place in the country before the global initiative. CBT modules were used to deliver technical IT topics. Additionally, a successful innovative pilot took place in the spring of 2001. This concerned the training of business English using imaginatively produced CD-ROMs that allowed links to an e-mail questioning facility and, through this means, provided tutor support for participants. Ironically, this material for English training to German nationals was produced by Auralog, a French company.

Given this experience, the German HR function was positive about global rollout. The country practice is committed and businesses are receptive and supportive. At the strategic level, Broening believes that the business will benefit from the improved quality of training material and especially the opportunity to gain access to worldwide methodology in the audit practice. In addition, there are benefits for staff development: Accessible Web-based learning maps or paths will help managers to understand how they can achieve promotion; recruitment and retention will be assisted if the firm acquires the reputation of adopting leading-edge learning technology. At the operational level, learning should no longer be dependent on time and place. Up to 80 percent of professionals in the German practice could be working at clients' premises, often in other cities, and organizing classroom training is logistically difficult. There are many advantages in allowing people to schedule their own learning. Improved monitoring and tracking of training should also become possible.

Some Important Issues

Earlier in this chapter some questions were raised on the cultural acceptability of learning materials produced for a global audience. Bob Blondin, chief learning strategist for Ernst & Young Intellinex, recognizes this problem. He sees three challenging areas as the EYLC proceeds.

The first issue concerns applicability from a technical standpoint. For example, how useful will material generated in the United States on taxation be to a tax specialist operating in the Nordic countries? The second is that of cultural acceptance. At the simplest level, idiomatic expressions must be avoided: The expression "hit a home run" in a leadership performance management module has little (or no) resonance outside the United States or Japan. Case studies need to be treated very carefully. Blondin uses the term *scrubbing* to describe the process of eliminating any potentially problematic content to produce a culturally neutral scenario.

The third issue concerns the language used in the material. All Ernst & Young professional staff are expected to have a working knowledge of business English—and (so far) this is the language of the Internet and e-learning. However, learners are most comfortable learning in their first language, so a second layer of complication will be added to the first layer of learning using technological means. It is quite feasible to translate material into other languages: All U.S. training material is translated into French for use in Quebec. Cost is the barrier, and a decision has been made to translate only when the population is large enough to justify this operation.

In Broening's view, because the material is developed outside of Germany, two types of problems will arise for employees in the German practice. The first concerns the sophistication of content. The German education system gives new entrants a good ground of theory, so some technical modules will be too elementary. Special laws apply in Germany (as elsewhere) on various technical topics that can be covered in tax-and-audit-training modules. The second problem concerns language. Most of the employees in the German practice understand business English, but this will not be sufficient. Language problems can be subtle, and because culture is grounded in language, increased language training, which demands time, will be required as part of the implementation program. Also under active consideration is the appointment of an e-learning mediator or coach to support learners who are experiencing difficulties.

The Global Challenge
From Blondin's perspective as the Intellinex vice president responsible for the project, several general problems have been identified:

> First, technology will always be an area of concern. There is a need to get from the application service provider (ASP) in the US to the desktop. Each country has its own technological topology and infrastructure. Secondly, different countries have different human resource information systems and, therefore, there is a need to extract information in different ways.

In Blondin's view, high-level sponsorship is critical but there must be an understanding of the significance of the change that is being sponsored: "People must be clear what they are sponsoring."

Another problem concerns how the Web site fits with the organizational structure. The U.K. practice was determined that, when the EYLC was launched, each individual (irrespective of level, discipline, function, or location) would have a portal and material that was meaningful to him or her. Ernst & Young's U.K. organization is complicated, and dealing with this complex issue was a challenge.

A further problem concerns the fit with other systems operating in the organization. Moreover, a business advisory firm has custody of a good deal of client-sensitive information. Access must reflect many security requirements, records must be kept up to date, and all legal data protection requirements must be observed.

Additionally, when global organizations are considering introducing e-learning to employees within the European Union, issues about data protection need to be addressed. There is still little insight into these issues. However, Ernst & Young, in the U.K. implementation, covered these issues even when data were being tranferred out of the EU's jurisdiction. Finola Harrington commented: "We realized during our project planning that as Intellinex would ultimately deploy e-learning for us across Europe that it was important that we considered the data protection issues and any other specific governance issues where data was being processed outside the EU on the firm's behalf."

A different set of issues—the organizational legacy—is subtle but equally, if not more, challenging. Des Woods, U.K. head of learning, offers the following insight: "I've spent as much time debating the organizational consequences of the shift to self-managed learning as I have on the deployment of the Web." Among the topics to be addressed are the shift in costs. "Money up front, delivery cheap" means that the way businesses allocate budgets and share investment costs is changed. Learning at the desk means that a new management perspective is required (and new time accounting codes must be created). The traditional channels for nominations for courses will change and the focus of control shift; management control in participation in training will become much more difficult. Relationships with existing suppliers of training will change, and those who manage them will require new skills.

Broening would agree. In her view, the problems in introducing e-learning lie not with technology itself but with the application of technology to learning ("the pedagogical and didactic uses of technology"). She argues that you cannot do everything with technology, and that where you use it must depend on your learning goals. You need to be clear where education in the sense of task-dependent learning is required, and where the need is for transmitting knowledge. According to Broening: "You must create a new architecture for learning in the organization. E-learning is not standalone, its limits must be understood and it must be integrated."

Such sentiments could stand as a summary for this whole book!

Author's Note: Thanks are due to Dr. Sylvia Broening, Finola Harrington, and Brenton Hague for their assistance with this case study.

Chapter 6

The Changing Role of the Trainer

"You've got to be careful if you don't know where you're going, because you might not get there."

In the introduction to this book, a target audience was identified as "those involved in directing, managing, or supporting the training function, irrespective of the role or title." The wider accountability for developing an organization's HR capital means that responsibility is far more dispersed.

This chapter is more specific in focus: It considers the role of the training manager or trainer in the organization. Designations vary— the word *learning* is starting to appear in job titles, such as chief learning officer. However, we are talking about the roles and responsibilities of someone whose primary activities are designed to enhance the knowledge, skills, and capabilities of individuals in the organization. How will these roles be affected, what activities should be undertaken, and what skills are required?

A starting point against which these perspectives can be reviewed is the discussion on the new paradigm, learner-centered interventions, that formed the conclusion of Chapter 3. This paradigm is now presented as Focus Point 22. It will be the focus of the job of the training manager and trainers of the future.

Chapter 5 ended on a discouraging note. The new technology, it was argued, offers training the opportunity to design and deliver interventions to suit learners' needs. However, at this stage, we simply do not know enough about how people learn in the new context.

> **_Focus Point 22: Learner-Centered Interventions_**
>
> A new paradigm will be based on learner-centered interventions. These will become a central accountability of the training manager and are characterized by:
>
> ♦ Emphasis on the learners and their acceptance of their responsibility
> ♦ A holistic (or integrated) approach to creating competitive advantage through people in the organization
> ♦ The need to ensure that resources are focused appropriately and managed effectively

There are huge opportunities for increasing the job satisfaction of the individual trainer.

Fortunately, when we look at the changing role of the trainer in this chapter, we can be much more positive. There are huge opportunities for enhancing the position of the profession and for increasing the job satisfaction of the individual trainer. The skill sets involved can be specified and identified and a start made. These skills sets are summarized in Proposition 16.

Proposition 16

Three distinct functional specialisms for trainers will evolve: design, delivery, and learner support.

Some implications for these functional specialisms are developed in the course of this chapter. It is helpful to begin this analysis with a practical distinction—that between the training professional (normally a training manager) who is working on the facilitation of a broader range of learning opportunities with individuals and groups, and those working on instructional development or delivery. This distinction has been expressed as follows:

Acting as a strategic facilitator involves taking a clear managerial responsibility for the overall provision of training in the organization and its effectiveness—in particular a responsibility for the development of the training culture.

In the alternative "deliverer" role, the training professional does not assume primary management responsibility for the training effort; such responsibility lies elsewhere in the organization, with either the human resource function or line management, or a combination of both. Instead the training professional is relatively detached and he or she offers a specialized service of advice, design and delivery, with the aim of meeting needs identified by those responsible for the management of the function.[1]

A new set of specialisms has emerged.

The potential gains from e-learning have increased the complexity and the focus of the role of the strategic facilitator (the training manager). As has been emphasized, that focus is now firmly on learner-centered interventions. The second role—specialized service of advice, design, and delivery (the trainer)—has also been dramatically altered: A new set of specialisms has emerged. Again, "training professional" will be used to encompass the training manager and the trainer.

Hard and Soft Technology

For both the strategic facilitator and the specialist trainer roles, Proposition 17 offers a useful starting point to consider the changes that follow from connectivity.

Proposition 17

A useful distinction can be made between hard technology and soft technology. The expertise of many trainers is in soft technology and this offers them an attractive future.

The concept of soft technology (and the distinction from hard technology) was introduced in Focus Point 15. Hard technology refers to the information and communication technology systems and the architecture of these systems as applied to learning (see Figure 2-2). Soft technology refers to those organizational activities that must be undertaken at all levels in an organization to embed that hard technology effectively.

One of the recurrent themes throughout this book is that technology is an enabler. Proposition 4, for example, states that there is a danger of becoming seduced by the functionality of the technology, rather than concentrating on its use. Proposition 12 states that e-learning will be most effective for the acquisition of knowledge and least effective where interpersonal interaction is needed for learning. Proposition 13 states that e-learning will be most effective as part of a systematic approach involving classroom and experiential learning with appropriate support.

Figure 6-1 develops the concept further by identifying the soft-technology components of a generalized e-learning system's architecture. Figure 6-1 is a parallel to the hard-technology components set out in Figure 2-2. Together, these figures can be of value in defining the issues that must be considered in implementing an e-learning solution.

The headings used in Figure 6-1 reflect many of the issues discussed in the case studies that are introduced throughout the book. To follow the approach used in Chapter 2, where hard technology was considered, the following definitions may assist:

♦ *Promotion*—the way that the system is marketed within the organization. This extends beyond the production of leaflets and posters. It can also involve familiarization training delivered to individuals at their desks.

♦ *Scope*—the applications of the learning system in the organization. What is it designed to achieve? Is it, for example, about getting learners to take more responsibility for their own development?

♦ *Fit*—the way in which the learning system relates to other HR activity, such as performance management or knowledge management.

FIGURE 6-1

E-learning system architecture: soft technology.

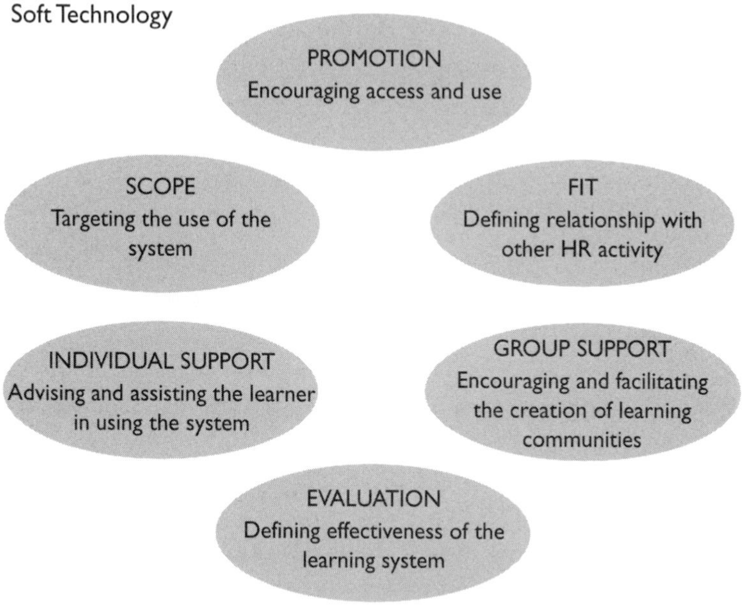

Soft Technology

PROMOTION
Encouraging access and use

SCOPE
Targeting the use of the
system

FIT
Defining relationship with
other HR activity

INDIVIDUAL SUPPORT
Advising and assisting the learner
in using the system

GROUP SUPPORT
Encouraging and facilitating
the creation of learning
communities

EVALUATION
Defining effectiveness of the
learning system

- *Individual support*—extends beyond the initial familiarization considered in *Promotion.* It embraces all of the ongoing activity designed to help learners take maximum advantage of the opportunities now available.
- *Group support*—the extent to which learning communities should be encouraged and supported. The term *e-moderating* will be used for this activity later in the chapter.
- *Evaluation*—a key feature of the trainer's role. The extent to which it has changed will be considered in a later section.

To emphasize, in e-learning, softer interventions that will be delivered by a skilled individual will always be important.

A well-rehearsed parody in the business world illustrates the continued role of the softer interventions. It goes as follows: E-business will be overtaken by m-business, which depends on information delivered through wireless technology (mobile phones). In turn, however, this will be superseded by s-business, which will make rapid advances, particularly in retail.

An s-business approach to purchasing clothes, for example, involves the following activities: An individual would enter a physical outlet and be presented with a range of alternatives; he or she would be able to try on the clothes for size and get an immediate appreciation of colors; other s-business outlets could be visited. These s-business outlets would be branded as "shops" and would offer a high-touch alternative to the high-tech approach of e-business. Venture capitalists are optimistic that the s-business model will succeed.

Getting the right balance between high tech (delivery through systems) and high touch (delivery through personal interaction) is recognized as a key element in all aspects of business activity in the connected economy. Figure 6-2 is taken from an internal Ernst & Young illustration that outlines the changing pattern of e-business in professional services. Today, a small proportion of the total market is exclusively high touch. In the future, the model will be more fragmented (or blurred): Some knowledge will be delivered using high-tech means, people will also be required to deliver knowledge using high touch, and there will be hybrid solutions (involving both technology and personal interventions) in between. This model will apply to training; the parallels are exact. The skills required of the professional will reflect the delivery requirements of the model.

FIGURE 6-2
E-business case—professional services.

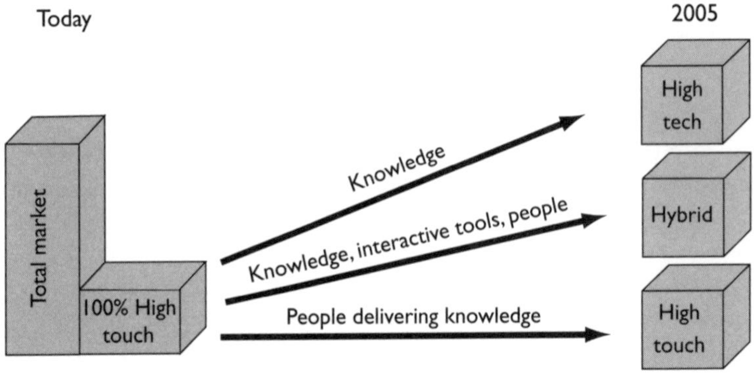

(Reproduced with permission of Ernst & Young.)

The Changing Skills: An ASTD View

In 1998, the ASTD published the results of an important study concerning a wide-ranging review of the challenge that the influx of learning development technologies posed for HR professionals:

> The ability to decide on and use an emerging array of learning technologies in a variety of roles is rapidly becoming a key set of required competencies for HRD professionals. Whether the HRD function is training, human performance improvement, or something else, it is increasingly evident that HRD departments must have members who are capable of using learning technologies for training and development. These capabilities ensure that the department can perform tasks ranging from advising on technology systems acquisition to designing and using specific technology applications to providing the logistical support often required for technology-based delivery. The training team must play a role in all of these activities, as well as in the design, development, and delivery of training using whatever technology mix is appropriate.[2]

The ASTD study identified eight distinct roles in the implementation of e-learning; these are reproduced in Focus Point 23. To an extent, they can be mapped to the roles discussed earlier in this chapter.

The first two roles, Human Resources Development (HRD) manager and analyst, relate to activities undertaken by strategic facilitators. This also applies to the evaluator role, though mastery of this activity is critical to all training professionals. The other ASTD roles can be clustered around the specialisms involved in Proposition 16 (three distinct functional specialisms for trainers will evolve: design, delivery, and learner support). *Design* embraces the ASTD's designer and developer roles. *Delivery* embraces both implementer and instructor. The ASTD's eighth role of organizational change agent embraces learning support, the third specialism in Proposition 16.

Design and Delivery

Where the literature and practice is strong is on the harder skills of ISD. This term was introduced in Chapter 3, and Figure 3-1 reproduces a table taken from the same ASTD report that considered the new roles for trainers just outlined.

Focus Point 23: Roles for Learning Technologies— The ASTD Analysis

Role	Description of the Role
HRD manager	Determines which learning technology, or combination of technologies, an organization should use to meet the comprehensive needs of the company. Decides when these technologies should be used and monitors the progress of all the other roles in the delivery process.
Analyst	Identifies performance gaps and recommends performance objectives that address the gaps. Determines if training is the proper intervention.
Designer	Determines what content, instructional methods, presentation methods and distribution methods will achieve the desired objectives and will suit the needs of the trainee population. Also creates the design document that will integrate all of these elements.
Developer	Uses the design document to create materials that are delivered via various presentation methods.
Implementer	Works with technical staff to set up and provide logistical support for technology devices. Also works with suppliers to produce and distribute electronic training materials.
Instructor	Facilitates learning either in a live broadcast or in an advanced technology classroom.
Evaluator	Measures the success of the source objectives and the effectiveness of the technology.
Organizational change agent	Helps the organization adapt to the new technology and see its value and benefits.

(Reproduced with permission from the American Society for Training and Development.[3])

There is a rich and continuing discipline of applying sound instructional principles to training. As long ago as 1946, educator and writer Edgar Dale introduced the "cone of experience." This has found its way into countless "train the trainers" sessions. Briefly, it states that people generally remember 10 percent of what they read, 20 percent of what they hear, 30 percent of what they see, 50 percent of what they hear and see, 70 percent of what they say and write, and 90 percent of what they say as they do a thing.

The ISD approach has been given new impetus as the technology available has become more sophisticated. Using a systems-processing approach provides the basis of a framework that leads to practical implementation.

According to author and consultant Deborah Schreiber:

> Distance and distributed education and training represent a process composed of multiple and diverse elements. These elements or components are associated with several categories, including the learner, instructor, learning environment, instructional delivery technology, and the culture of the organization providing the training.
>
> Applying the systems processing approach of ISD to the development and delivery of distance and distributed training provides a strategy for understanding the roles of the student located at a remote site and the instructor designing materials to be delivered at a distance over some technical medium. A systems processing strategy enables investigation of the relationships amongst the various elements of the process, including, in addition to the student and instructor, the learning environment (for example, site planning for a satellite broadcast, or desktop access), the instructional technology (compressed video or Internet), and the culture of the institution or agency (including level of organizational technology capability for providing distance training).[4]

For any training professional with an ambition to specialize in e-learning design, the message is simple: Investigate the literature. Two books are recommended: *Distance Training,* by Schreiber and Berge,[5] from which the preceding quotation is taken and *The ASTD Handbook of Training Design and Delivery.*[6] Regular articles and discussions also appear in the ASTD's magazine *T +D.* A valuable volume published in the United Kingdom is Judith Christian-Carter's *Mastering Instructional Design in TBT.*[7]

Two final points should be made on design and delivery in e-learning. The first concerns design for the Web and the second the other skills of delivery. Given the current growth of e-business, effective Web design has, of course, become a hot topic. Much of the current debate is focused on the B2C sites and B2B sites. Learning systems that concern B2E interface have not received the same attention. Nevertheless, the same principles apply, and a set of best practice rules is emerging. It seems sensible to accept, for example, that a user's main concern is getting access to the information immediately. A standard sequence, therefore, would be first to decide on content and then to work out navigation. For those wishing to pursue this aspect of design further, the work of Jakob Nielsen, who has researched and written extensively on the Web and usability, is recommended. His recent book is called *Designing Web Usability,* and his Web site is *www.useit.com.*[8]

The point to be made on skills of delivery is straightforward. Proposition 13 argues that e-learning will be most effective as part of a systematic approach involving classroom and experiential learning with appropriate support (blended learning). The traditional skills of the trainer must never be overlooked—even if they are delivered in a different context.

Supporting Learners: Digital Collaboration

As should be apparent from the arguments advanced so far, developing effective learner support may be the major challenge facing the training profession. The connected economy allows learner-centered interventions to be designed and delivered; this will require support for individual learners across a range of activities. As suggested in the previous chapter, the topic is underresearched. The United States has a strong tradition of ISD but is less advanced in this softer area.

However, what can be stated with confidence is that there is a body of knowledge on discrete activities (or elements) involved in learner support. Taken together with a more effective research base, they could amount to a new discipline. Certainly there are opportunities for individual trainers to identify and acquire the new skill set.

Developing effective learner support may be the major challenge.

Broadly, these skills can be divided into two categories: those that are related immediately to the delivery of training using technology, and those that take place independently of any e-learning activity. This second category is the more traditional role, which is well developed in the literature.

The work of Elliott Masie offers much guidance on the first category. He uses the term *digital collaboration* to describe the situation in which:

> two or more people [are] working or learning together, separated by distance and perhaps time.

> Digital collaboration will turn our desktops, laptops, cell phones and handheld/wearable devices into rich media communicators. Our corporate networks will increasingly be used for collaboration and communication, as well as transactions and content delivery.[9]

Providing support for learners participating in digital collaboration involves a range of activities. These include support for access to technology, pre-learning activities, and post-learning reinforcement. One aspect where there is a developing literature is the moderation or facilitation of online discussion groups. Much of the experience that has been gained to date has arisen in an educational context. Significant expertise has been developed as a result of interventions designed to enhance learner experience in universities using modern distance-learning techniques. One example is outlined in the next section.

Supporting Learners: E-Moderating

Gilly Salmon, a senior lecturer at the UK Open University Business School, has offered a most useful practical contribution in her book

E-Moderating: The Key to Teaching and Learning Online.[10] Most help-fully, and in the spirit of knowledge sharing, she has established an e-moderating home page at *http://oubs.open.ac.uk/e-moderating.*

Salmon describes the e-moderator as someone who presides over an electronic meeting or conference. Such an activity demands a different awareness and approach from a face-to-face meeting and requires a rather wider range of expertise. Her preferred term to describe much of the activity is *computer-mediated conferencing* (CMC):

> CMC provides a way of sending messages to a group of users, using computers for storage and mediation. A computer, somewhere, holds all the messages until a participant is ready to log on and access them, so on-line conferences do not require participants to be available at a particular time.[11]

(This is a form of asynchronous activity; see Focus Point 17.)

Three types of technology are involved in CMC: a server and software system, a terminal or PC for each user, and a telecommunications system to connect the computers to the server. This hard technology will doubtless increase dramatically in functionality. The introduction of video clips showing the individual talking is an obvious development. The soft technology requires skills and management.

In her book and associated Web site, Salmon presents a five-stage model drawn from her research. The broad headings of these stages are access and motivation, online socialization, information exchange, knowledge construction, and development. If these stages progress effectively, a community in which individuals gain and share knowledge can be built. The tasks of the e-moderator vary and evolve at each stage (from welcoming and encouraging at the first stage, for example, to supporting and responding at the last). A set of online competencies for e-moderators is developed from this analysis and presented and explored in her book.

CMC may manifest itself differently in the corporate environment from in the academic. Online communities may, for example, have a shorter life expectancy in the corporate environment (they may be focused on a particular project); the motivation of participants may be different. However, the importance of effective moderation will remain an issue and there is much to be learned.

Consider the following comments from Professor David Asch, who participated in a group that bridged a corporate and academic community:

> First some general observations. There are a limited number of contributors in each of the sections; the discussion leaders of each seem to be trying hard to engage individuals in the debate; of course I do not know how many of the others are "lurking" and not contributing (as I was). Second, after an initial flurry of activity little seems to be happening. I suspect this is because of a lack of focus, or perhaps a lack of interest, or maybe because people involved find that the "discussions" appear to lack structure and direction.
>
> I must admit to finding the discussions (of potentially very interesting topics) somewhat uninspiring. I do not know how the groups were set up or what they were supposed to do. But on the basis of what I've read, and the quality of that, it did appear that more focus and direction would have helped to lift the level of debate and hence to engage more people if they could see some benefit for themselves from involvement. I would suspect that given the nature of the people, the importance of the topic, and the importance of learning that the process may have been facilitated by being somewhat more directive not only in terms of content and development of outcomes, but perhaps more importantly in terms of process and timescales.

Managing learner-centered intervention is a new discipline. However, jobs are emerging, and Focus Point 24 is a reproduction of an earlier job description of one of the new roles. This is set out in a summary of an e-moderating job at learndirect, the brand name for the UK University for Industry (Ufi).

Supporting Learners

Earlier in this chapter, it was emphasized that the traditional skills of the trainer must never be overlooked. The ability to deliver material to an audience, to manage interaction in the classroom, and to build the learner's self-confidence on a one-to-one basis remain key skills

Focus Point 24: E-Moderating: Learndirect Job Outlines

The Job

Reporting to the e-learning manager, you will have responsibility for the delivery of high-quality learner support of a non-subject-specific nature. You will be instrumentally involved in determining reasonable learner support requirements and will work closely with your e-learning facilitator colleagues to provide support to match these requirements. You will provide much of this support synchronously within the learndirect online working environment. You will need to work flexibly, at various times of the day and not necessarily to uniform work patterns. Your role will involve some evening and weekend work.

Prime Responsibilities

1   Implement Ufi's innovative learner support model, both nationally and throughout the hub network.
2   Proactively support online learners who require motivating and who are experiencing simple problems.
3   Signpost learners to other services providing in-depth support or advice.
4   Work with the team to implement and update databases of frequently asked questions (FAQs).
5   Facilitate national learner conferences within the Ufi Web site to encourage and develop usage of the support services.
6   Support online tutors and facilitators from Ufi hubs using the online tutor conference.
7   Train online tutors and facilitators as necessary.
8   Administer the online tools.
9   Develop and implement ideas for the dynamic learning Web site with other members of the distributed learning team.
10   Help in developing Ufi standards for learner support.
11   Monitor the application of Ufi standards for learner support.
12   Identify and share good practice in learner support.

Qualifications, Skills and Experience

Essential

1   Educated to degree level or equivalent.
2   Minimum of two years' experience of face-to-face tutoring and facilitation or other learning support role.

3   Sound understanding of the differences between online and
    face-to-face tutoring.
4   Highly developed interpersonal skills.
5   Experience of using common computer applications and e-mail.
6   Experience in planning, developing and organizing training.
7   Proven ability to contribute as a team member to group out-
    comes.

(Reproduced with thanks to the University for Industry.)

of value to the organization. The arrival of e-learning simply means
that they will be delivered in a new context.

One of the points used to clarify the concept of learner-centered
interventions in Focus Point 22 was "emphasis on the learners and
their acceptance of their responsibility." A whole series of approaches,
techniques, and mechanisms has been developed to assist in this process. All fall into the broad category of softer interventions. There is
much literature available on these approaches.

Some illustrations, taken from current practice at Ernst & Young,
UK, may assist.[12] The first is drawn from the implementation process
for E&Y Learning Connection in the United Kingdom (see Chapter
5). The project team prepared extensive communications for staff
and, in particular, counseling managers (managers with line responsibility for staff performance and development) on the importance of
and approach to the support of learners. The team regarded this as a
significant change management exercise. The key elements for the
counselor to consider were identified as:

♦ Understanding how learners would need support to orientate
  themselves around the new system.
♦ Understanding how learners would find learning offerings that
  were relevant to their needs; this was picked up in the Web-based
  orientation product.
♦ Having the counseling manager ensure that there were regular
  interventions with the learner so that both parties would understand that learning at the desk is admissible and as important as
  learning off the job.

Brenton Hague, the Ernst & Young senior manager responsible for communications for EY Learning Connection, commented: "We were keen to use the technology solution to enable the change in our learning culture. The aim was to create a positive environment where a learner takes full responsibility for his/her learning."

A second illustration taken from Ernst & Young concerns the clarification of some of the processes involved in one-to-one learning support. Focus Point 25 offers a set of definitions, which may inevitably differ from those preferred by some of the case study organizations cited in this book.

A third illustration concerns one approach used in group support: the encouragement of self-managed learning groups. Focus Point 26 outlines the proposition used at Ernst & Young to facilitate the estab-

---

Focus Point 25: Some Definitions of the Helping Process

Coaching, counseling, and mentoring are all regarded as "helping processes," and all can assist in accelerating the learning and performance of staff. They are defined as follows:

- *Coaching*—a process in which a manager, through direct discussion and guided activity, helps a colleague to solve a problem or a task more effectively than would otherwise have been the case. It also includes the process of producing personal development and action plans. Coaching is task centered in that it focuses on the work processes, appropriate behaviors, and actions the individual needs to take to improve performance.
- *Counseling*—a process that helps the individual resolve personal issues that impede effective work performance or the development of new skills and attitudes. The style of delivery is usually nondirective/neutral. Counseling is person centered in that it focuses on whatever the issues may be for an individual.
- *Mentoring*—a process that helps a person handle significant transitions in responsibility and/or status. It provides advice on such issues as the suitability of career goals, personal strategies, and tactics. There will normally be a significant difference in seniority between mentors and those assisted.

Focus Point 26: Self-Managed Learning Groups

A self-managed learning group brings together a number of people with a similar broad objective (for example, partnership entry). With the assistance of a coaching specialist they form a group, develop an agenda, and decide how to organize themselves to move forward.

The objectives of such a group for the individual are defined as follows:

♦ To enable individuals to produce a tailored program—learning goals, strategies, methods, tactics—to suit them
♦ To help individuals maintain momentum by providing challenges, reviewing progress, and providing feedback
♦ To raise self-awareness
♦ To provide useful content—but not a talking shop

The added-value outcomes are finding out:

♦ How to learn from experience
♦ How to operate in ambiguous situations
♦ How to measure one's progress
♦ How to develop one's career

The principles of operation are to:

♦ Show interest in others.
♦ Be open to others.
♦ Be open with others.
♦ Expect achievement.
♦ Assess achievement.
♦ Expect agreements to be kept.
♦ Challenge oneself and others.

lishment of such groups. The underlying process is set out in Figure 6-3.

Finally, one obvious advantage of e-learning is that it allows training interventions to be made much more transparent for the learner. These interventions can be promoted as learning systems (not to be confused with the narrow use of the term—as a vendor's product—in

FIGURE 6-3
Self-managed learning.

The Process

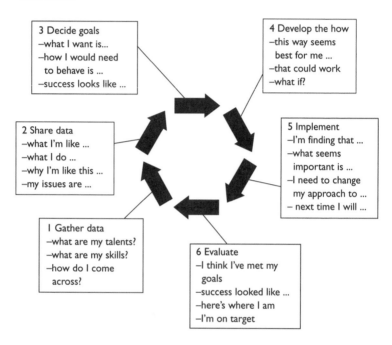

3 Decide goals
–what I want is...
–how I would need
to behave is ...
–success looks like ...

4 Develop the how
–this way seems
best for me ...
–that could work
–what if?

2 Share data
–what I'm like ...
–what I do ...
–why I'm like this ...
–my issues are ...

5 Implement
–I'm finding that ...
–what seems
important is ...
–I need to change
my approach to ...
– next time I will ...

1 Gather data
–what are my talents?
–what are my skills?
–how do I come
across?

6 Evaluate
–I think I've met my
goals
–success looked like ...
–here's where I am
–I'm on target

(Reproduced with permission of Ernst & Young.)

Chapter 2). An illustrative learning system, for senior Ernst & Young staff who are aiming for partnership, is set out as Figure 6-4.

E-learning allows training interventions to be made much more transparent for the learner.

Regardless of the approach used, providing effective learner support will be a critical professional accountability for the future. Opportunities are evident in instructional design and development. This chapter has demonstrated the wide range and scope that e-learning has

FIGURE 6-4

Core learning system for partner track.

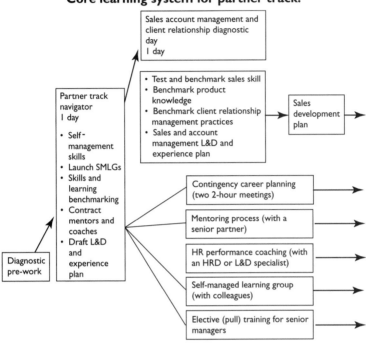

(Reproduced with permission of Ernst & Young.)

created for trainers. If we fail to take advantage, we will have no one to blame but ourselves.

Notes

1   M. Sloman, *A Handbook for Training Strategy,* 2nd ed. (Aldershot, U.K.: Gower, 1999), 233.

2   G. M. Piskurich and E. S. Sanders, *ASTD Models for Learning Technologies: Roles, Competencies and Outputs* (Alexandria, Va.: American Society for Training and Development, 1998), 26.

3   Ibid.

4   D. A. Schreiber and Z. L. Berge, eds., *Distance Training* (San Francisco: Jossey-Bass, 1998), 27.

5   Ibid.

6   G. M. Piskurich, P. Beckschi, and B. Hall, *The ASTD Handbook of Training Design and Delivery* (New York: McGraw-Hill, 2000), 39.

7   J. Christian-Carter, *Mastering Instructional Design in TBT* (London: Chartered Institute of Personnel and Development, 2001).

8   J. Nielsen, *Designing Web Usability* (Indianapolis: New Riders, 2000).

9   E. Masie, "Digital Collaboration: The Next Wave of Corporate Technology," *Learning Decisions,* June 2000.

10 G. Salmon, *E-Moderating: The Key to Teaching and Learning Online* (London: Kogan Page, 2000).

11 Ibid., 15–16.

12 I am grateful to my colleagues Des Woods and Mike Laws for permission to reproduce their work.

Chapter 7

Training in Transition

When asked by a waitress whether he wanted his pizza cut into four or eight pieces: "Better make it four—I don't think I can eat eight."

Changes caused by connectivity will be far-reaching. The whole training industry could be altered, and it is difficult to predict what steady state will be attained. At the heart of this lies the economic forces that were discussed in Chapter 1. These are summarized in Focus Point 27.

The previous chapter looked at the way the skill set of trainers will change. The implication throughout was that the trainer would be working in a corporate role or offering brought-in services as a consultant. Inspection of the ASTD analysis of roles set out in Focus Point 23 shows that many of these functions could be delivered from either of these standpoints.

This chapter widens the analysis beyond the role of the individual. It considers the potential implications for the training industry as a whole by illustrating the power of changing market relationships. It then focuses on strategic resource management—reemphasizing the importance of effective evaluation.

Changing Market Relationships

Focus Point 27 contains a generic list of components of the new business model that will emerge as a result of connectivity. All could apply, to a greater or lesser degree, to the training industry. Indeed, many activities reflecting these forces have already been put in place. Some initiatives have proved successful, some less successful; with

Focus Point 27: Key Components of New Business Models

♦ Low-cost access to global markets/suppliers
♦ Reduced marketing and sales costs for businesses
♦ 24-hour shopping and reduced costs for customers
♦ Elimination of traditional intermediaries and emerging new intermediaries
♦ Further/cheaper connections between businesses, leading to reduced costs and increased agility in the supply chain
♦ Enhanced communication with internal stakeholders leading to faster responses and improved speed to market
♦ New entrants into markets supplying completely new offerings, potentially eliminating existing players in that market

(Reproduced by permission of Ernst & Young.)

others it is too early to tell. What is beyond doubt is that the traditional boundaries and relationships between suppliers could disappear or be blurred. Some illustrations may assist.

One early initiative was the establishment in 1995 of the executive education network. This involved a consortium of leading business schools (including Wharton, Penn State, and Babson) and a specialist communications company. The aim was to offer high-quality business school teaching to corporate clients. Managers assembled in classrooms, received synchronous classroom tuition via satellite, and were supported by local tutors or business school specialists.

Despite its superficial attraction—top-quality business education delivered locally—the initiative did not develop. According to some of the business school staff involved, there were late cancellations and substitutions; too many participants did not undertake their prereading. Moreover, those participants who received the teaching by satellite felt at a disadvantage compared with those who were located with the lead tutor. The tutors in the satellite classrooms were often untrained or simply absent.[1]

A second illustration concerns the current initiatives under way at Harvard Business School. Harvard has a powerful reputation and hence an immensely strong brand. To many, the key to Harvard's success is the reputation of its faculty, the quality and practical relevance of its research, and its ability to teach using the case study method. Harvard's executive education courses can therefore command a considerable premium. In summer 2000, Harvard Business School Publishing launched High Performance Management On-Line. This is an intranet/Internet tool using multimedia technology offering interactive case studies. A number of *Harvard Business Review* articles are built in as a resource library. The twenty topic areas include exercising power and influence, managing change, and even the softer skills of coping with stress and emotion. Does this initiative dilute Harvard's brand, or is it leveraging its competitive advantage into a new market? Time will tell. What is important in the context of this discussion is a recognition that one of the most senior players in executive education is prepared to compete in a different way. Given the global reach of the Internet, it would be a brave second-division business school that would invest in a product that competes directly with Harvard.

It would be a brave second-division business school that would invest in a product that competes directly with Harvard.

A third illustration was the announcement made by the Massachusetts Institute of Technology (MIT) in April 2001. MIT stated its intention of making the materials for nearly all of its courses freely available on the Internet over the following year. The chair of the MIT faculty, Steve Lerman, argued that the project stemmed both from enthusiasm for the opportunities that the Internet affords for widespread sharing of educational ideas and from concern over the growing "privatization of knowledge." He noted that many universities, including MIT, see the Internet as a means of delivering revenue-generating distance education. But, as was noted in a press release, "we also need to take advantage of the tremendous power of the Internet to build on the tradition at MIT and in American higher education of open dissemination of educational materials and innovations in teaching."

Changing market relations are particularly apparent in the interface between corporate organizations and university business schools. One manifestation of this change is the emergence of the corporate university, which is considered in the next section. Another example is contained in the first case study at the end of the chapter. Duke University Place and Space shows how a highly respected business school has developed its own technology to extend its reach and improve its service to students.

The Corporate University

Corporate universities have received a great deal of attention and may offer an attractive way forward under the right circumstances. However, the concept should not be embraced without some critical analysis. Cynically, it could be suggested that (with the exception of accreditation of programs) a corporate university could be no more than either a more modern manifestation of the traditional internal corporate college—the residential training establishments that were so fashionable in the 1970s and 1980s—or a rebadging and repromotion of a company's internal training department.

A healthy skepticism is a vital attribute at this time of transition.

There is a grain of truth in such a view—a healthy skepticism is a vital attribute of the observer's armory at this time of transition. Certainly, the corporate university is an attractive option for only the more confident organization.

Two definitions of corporate universities were offered in a recent U.K. report.[2]

> A corporate university is formed when a corporation seeks to relate
> its training and development strategies to its business strategy by co-

ordination and integration and by the development of intellectual capital within the organization in pursuit of its corporate aims and objectives.

A corporate university is an internal structure designed to improve individual and business performance by ensuring that the learning and knowledge of a corporation is directly connected to its business strategy. A corporate university's students are drawn from its employees. It has the capacity to offer formal accreditation for some of the learning it provides.

A useful reference site on current development is the Corporate University Xchange (*www.corpu.com*). According to the Xchange, there are more than 2,000 corporate universities in the United States (up from 400 in 1986). Of the Fortune 500 companies, 40 percent have invested in a corporate university. The average cost is 2 percent of the company's payroll.

One attractive feature of many corporate universities is the opportunity for greater collaboration between the educational establishment and the corporate organization. Such collaboration can, of course, take place much more easily in the connected economy. An illustration in the United Kingdom, the Cap Gemini Ernst & Young Virtual Business School, is the subject of the second case study presented at the end of this chapter.

The Changing Supply Chain

The concept of a supply or value chain for training was outlined in Chapter 4 (see Figure 4-3). It was argued that those responsible for training should consider the chain that applies in their organization. In the context of the present chapter, it should be recognized that each of the players in the training industry must consider the value that they add. To survive they must understand that the market is changing and that transparency of information will drive down costs. It may be some time before the full impact of current forces becomes apparent. However, for the longer term, Proposition 18 can be advanced with confidence.

Proposition 18

Any part of the training supply chain that does not add value will disappear. Other parts could well become commodity products.

Consider, for example, the first column in Figure 4-3, the provision of raw material or content. Here, as has been noted, Harvard and MIT, among others, have made significant interventions in the market. More generally, despite an overall attempt to create a mystique, most of the soft-skills training elements are straightforward; the tools and techniques used in, say, performance feedback, interviewing, or facilitation do not vary much from trainer to trainer. One of the standard pieces of business guidance in coping with the changes brought about by connectivity is "Give your product away free. Make your money through services." Basic training content could, on this basis, become a commodity. The premium is to be gained from effective customization or delivery—especially in the classroom. In other words, for the smaller training consultancy, the future may lie in high touch (one-to-one or group delivery) rather than high technology.

This obviously poses a tremendous challenge for all external training consultants. The third and fourth case studies set out at the end of this chapter show how two consultancies that offer very different training products and services—Globecon and CCC/The Mentoring Group—have developed effective strategies that recognize the new realities.

Changing relationships across the supply or value chain give rise to new opportunities. They create new market spaces, to use the term in vogue. The establishment and activities of LearnShare, a consortium created to share and improve access to learning products and services, offer an interesting example of a different sort of training organization and form the basis of the final case study at the end of the chapter.

Changing relationships across the supply or value chain will also, however, give rise to a whole range of problems. Many of these are still to emerge, but one that can be firmly identified concerns copyright and access. If the basic "knowledge" components are made available over the intranet (and are also used in the classroom), who will own the intellectual property? Once again, it is the business and commercial drivers that will determine the agenda. The current formulation used in Ernst & Young's invitation to tender is set out in Focus Point 28. It may assist corporate organizations that use outsourced training organizations as the main means of delivery as they consider their contract procedures.

Strategic Resource Management

Irrespective of the changing relationships across the value chain, resource allocation will remain an issue of key importance. The collection and analysis of effective economic measures (or metrics) will remain an essential role for the training function. For example, Elliott Masie has offered the following formats for expressing e-learning budget figures: "Cost per new hire for stage one training; Cost per virtual course; Cost per employee for infrastructure; Cost per product release; Cost per year for learning management service. These are just a few of the metrics that we see popping up in the budget section of strategies."[3]

**Focus Point 28: Extract from Ernst & Young
Invitation to Tender**

10.   Intellectual property

The successful bidder must confirm acceptance of Sections 10.1, 10.2, and 10.3.

10.1 Any Ernst & Young models, single frames, tools, and so forth shared with the successful bidder must not be disclosed to a third party.

10.2 Any general models and outlines on training approaches (such as could be placed on the intranet) will remain the property of Ernst & Young.

10.3 Any specific classroom materials will remain the property of the training consultant but will be made available to Ernst & Young to be used outside the UK at an agreed-upon fee.

The objective of effective deployment of resources is not altered by the introduction of e-learning. However, as Proposition 19 suggests, the focus may shift.

Proposition 19

Time, not money, will become a scarce resource. Monitoring of use and evaluation of effectiveness will become critically important.

The phrase *work intensive* is often used to characterize modern society. For many people, work is interesting, fulfilling, demanding, but exhausting: There is always something else of value to do.

Proposition 19 should not be taken to suggest that expenditure on training no longer matters. Appropriate financial disciplines must apply to day-to-day budgetary control; investment decisions (increasingly concerned with the purchase of technology-based systems) must be subjected to the appropriate rigorous analysis. What the proposition does is draw a further inference from the new paradigm that formed the conclusion of Chapter 3—the move to learner-centered interventions.

Time for individual learning competes with other organizational demands.

If the focus is shifted to learners, and efforts are concentrated on ways to make them acquire skills and knowledge in the most efficient way, their time becomes the scarce resource. Time for individual learning competes with other organizational demands: time for client contact and selling, creative time to develop new products, time to develop staff, time for general administration. Increasingly, excessive organizational demands are competing with personal and domestic needs. There is a demand for an appropriate work/life balance. The ability of the connected economy to deliver training material to the learner "any time, any place" poses an obvious danger of a further intrusion into personal space ("I'll try to fit it in over the weekend").

Since for the learner time is the critical resource, in accordance with the new paradigm, it must also become the critical resource for the organization. Time must become a focus of evaluation interventions. Here the new connectivity offers a huge benefit: behavior and usage analysis, which is one element in many e-learning systems. This is the ability to automatically generate information on how much any individual uses a system. In short, learner-centered measurement becomes feasible. In my experience at Ernst & Young, this ability to monitor usage was considered by senior management to be of considerable benefit. Focus Point 29 discusses how the concept of clickstream data could be used to assist the effectiveness of training.

This learner-centered measurement should be placed in the overall framework of training evaluation. The most common evaluation framework adopted by training practitioners, the Kirkpatrick model, offers four levels of evaluation:

♦ *Reaction*—how well did training participants like the program?
♦ *Learning*—what knowledge (principles, facts, and techniques) did participants gain from the program?
♦ *Behavior*—what positive changes in participants' job behavior stemmed from the training program?
♦ *Results*—what were the training program's organizational effects in terms of reduced costs, improved quality of work, increased quantity of work, and so forth.[4]

Kirkpatrick, then, suggests that evaluation can be implemented at a series of different levels. An important gain from technology is that participant responses are easy to collect electronically. This requires the design and implementation of appropriate systems. Focus Point 30 contains a suite of participant feedback questionnaires for Web-based courses designed for use in Ernst & Young courses.[5] Examination of these forms indicates that they do generate some information on higher-level evaluation, but here much of the feedback should also be collected by questionnaire-based interview. For an outline of this approach, see the author's previous work.[6]

Focus Point 29: Clickstream Data

When people explore a Web site, their mouse clicks generate data that reflect their behavior. This information is called *clickstream data*. Proposition 2 argued that the drivers of Internet activity and development are business and commercial. These will shape and foreshadow developments in training. This proposition applies to the importance of clickstream data. Commercial organizations are using the data to learn how to design sites, how to make them user-friendly, how to market them, and how to personalize pages.

Commercial data that could be tracked typically include the following:

◆ Where did a visitor first land on a site?
◆ What attracted the visitor to the site?
◆ How many pages were viewed and in what order?
◆ How long did the visitor spend on each site?

For the commercial Internet company, the potential value of such clickstream data is evident. It can be used to determine advertising strategy. It can also be used to influence site design. The latter is most immediately analogous to the requirements of effective training. The aim is to attract learners to a site, make it easy to navigate, and thus promote efficient learning.

A whole collection of packages has been developed to assist with clickstream analysis for business Internet sites. Similar packages will doubtless be developed as learning systems become more popular. The issue facing those responsible for training will then be to determine what specific information will be of value to improve the opportunities for the learner.

Before this discussion on resource management concludes, one other difference that could result from e-learning should be noted. This concerns user reaction to a poor training experience. An important distinction is that an adverse reaction to course-based training can lead to complaints, whereas an adverse reaction to e-learning can lead to embarrassment. If people spend three days on a course (remember, time is the scarce resource) that was perceived to be a waste of time,

Focus Point 30: Participant Feedback Form

Please mark the box that best describes your level of satisfaction using the scale below

5	4	3	2	1	N/A
Strongly agree	Agree	Neither agree nor disagree	Disagree	Strongly disagree	Not applicable

LEARNING EFFECTIVENESS

1 I clearly understood the course objectives.   5 4 3 2 1 N/A

2 The course objectives were relevant to my   5 4 3 2 1 N/A
   needs.

3 The course was appropriate for me, given   5 4 3 2 1 N/A
   my knowledge and experience.

4 The knowledge and/or skills gained through   5 4 3 2 1 N/A
   this course are directly applicable to my
   job.

5 Overall, this course was an effective learn-   5 4 3 2 1 N/A
   ing experience.

6 List what you liked best about this learning
   experience.

   _____

   _____

   _____

   _____

   _____

After completing this program, I am confident that I can meet the following objectives . . .
(The following examples are objectives from Supply Chain 101)

1 Articulate key leading practices in supply   5 4 3 2 1 N/A
   chain management.

2 Identify supply chain metrics and value   5 4 3 2 1 N/A
   propositions.

3 Assist in the completion of a supply chain   5 4 3 2 1 N/A
   current state assessment.

4   Mine for knowledge and learn how to find   5 4 3 2 1 N/A
    resources (e.g. the supply chain power-
    pack) that can assist in the support supply
    chain engagements.

COURSE DESIGN

1   The course content was logically organized.   5 4 3 2 1 N/A

2   The course content was clearly written.   5 4 3 2 1 N/A

3   The use of audio enhanced my learning   5 4 3 2 1 N/A
    experience.

4   The course activities reinforced the con-   5 4 3 2 1 N/A
    tent.

5   The length of this course was . . .
                    ☐ Too long   ☐ Just right   ☐ Too short

COURSE DELIVERY

1   I was able to access this course when   5 4 3 2 1 N/A
    needed it.

2   The delivery method(s) used in this course   5 4 3 2 1 N/A
    was an effective way for me to learn the
    subject matter.

3   The amount of time it took me to access   5 4 3 2 1 N/A
    this course was acceptable.

4   It was easy to navigate through the Web-   5 4 3 2 1 N/A
    based learning product to find the informa-
    tion I needed.

5   These features were helpful and informa-
    tive.

    a) Help   5 4 3 2 1 N/A
    b) Site map   5 4 3 2 1 N/A
    c) Progress report   5 4 3 2 1 N/A
    e) Other (please list) 5 4 3 2 1 N/A

6   The setting in which I took this course was a(n):
    (Check appropriate box)

    a) office   ☐
    b) hotel   ☐
    c) client's office   ☐

d) home   ☐
e) other (please specify)   ☐

7   The setting (e.g. office, hotel, client's office, 5 4 3 2 1 N/A
    home) in which I took this course was ap-
    propriate.

ANTICIPATED IMPACT

Questions 1 and 2 require that you express your answer in increments of 10%.

1   What percentage of your total working time do you or will
    you spend on tasks that require the skills/knowledge pre-
    sented in this course?   _____%

2   Considering your work tasks, what percentage of the knowl-
    edge/skills presented in this program did you have a working
    knowledge of . . .

    a) before this course?   _____%
    b) after this course?   _____%

3   List two to three tasks, activities or responsibilities to which
    you plan to apply the skills and knowledge you gained from
    this course:

    a) _____
    b) _____
    c) _____

4   List ways in which your job performance will improve as a
    result of taking this course.

    a) _____
    b) _____
    c) _____

OPPORTUNITY FOR IMPROVEMENTS

1   List any barriers that may prevent you from using the knowl-
    edge and skills gained from this course.

    _____
    _____
    _____

2   List any enablers that would help you use the knowledge and
    skills you gained from this course more effectively.

    _____

    _____

    _____

3   List what you liked least about this course.

    _____

    _____

    _____

4   List any changes in content, delivery, formatting, etc. that
    would improve this course.

    _____

    _____

    _____

they may well articulate their reaction forcefully. The training manager/HR manager can expect a strongly worded e-mail or telephone conversation.

At present, and this could pass, an adverse reaction to Internet/intranet training may be conveniently forgotten. Assume that the learner is expected to access a module at his or her convenience (asynchronous training). If the experience is unfavorable (because of difficult access, bad navigation, or inappropriate content, for example), the module will not be revisited. Certainly in the current climate the learner may well lack the confidence to complain. It is in all parties' interests—the trainer's and the learner's—to say nothing at the time. Effective learner support is needed in order to ensure that this problem does not arise or that it is dealt with effectively after the event.

This chapter has focused on the economic forces affecting the training industry; the previous chapter focused on the role of the individual. The conclusions from both are positive: The prospects for capable individuals and quality consultancies are good. We all have reason to be optimistic. For those who are positive, embrace change, and can learn new skills, an exciting future beckons. The starting point is to ask, "Where can I add value?" As Aristotle reportedly said: "Where your talents and the needs of the world cross, there lies your vocation."

Notes

1 J. A. Byrne, "Virtual b-Schools," *Business Week,* October 23, 1995, 64–8. My thanks to my friends at Penn State, especially Al Vicere, for the additional insights.

2 Department for Education and Employment, the Campaign for Learning and the Further Education Development Agency, "The Future of Corporate Learning" (London: Department of Trade and Industry, 2000), 7.

3 From *Learning Decisions,* September 2000, 6.

4 D. L. Kirkpatrick, *Evaluating Training Programs* (Alexandria, Va.: American Society for Training and Development, 1975).

5 I am grateful to Bob Blondin and Bill Diffley of the U.S. practice of Ernst & Young for their permission to reproduce these questionnaires.

6 M. Sloman, *A Handbook for Training Strategy,* 2nd ed. (Aldershot, U.K.: Gower, 1999), 194–99.

PLACE AND SPACE AT DUKE CORPORATE EDUCATION

Duke Corporate Education (Duke CE) was formed on July 1, 2000. It is an offshoot of the well-known Fuqua School of Business at Duke University, North Carolina. Fuqua consistently achieves a top five position in published rankings of business schools. Duke University remains the major shareholder in Duke CE, which was established as a separate company to deliver executive education and associated consultancy to corporate clients. Since the creation of Duke CE, the parent Fuqua School continues open enrollment programs and maintains close links with Duke CE providing faculty input and other support. In its first year of operation, Duke CE was recognized by a recent *Financial Times* survey as the number two business school in the world for delivering custom executive education programs, many of which encompass the Place and Space approach.

For some time, Duke has recognized the potential importance of distance learning, and subsequently e-learning, in the delivery of management and executive education as a way of leveraging and extending the highly regarded Duke brand. As well as the advantages of the brand, Duke CE can claim a competitive edge based on a distinctive model of e-learning called Place and Space.

Place and Space

Duke's approach to e-learning was initially developed in the mid-1990s to serve the dispersed learning needs of the students in the Global MBA. It has subsequently been extended, following the formation of Duke CE, to executive education, which serves the needs of corporate clients. Place and Space, as the approach is termed, can be regarded as a form of blended learning—a view that e-learning will be most effective when it is part of an overall strategy involving the classroom and on-the-job workplace learning. By using an extended academic faculty, drawn from Duke and elsewhere, Duke CE can deliver blended, customized learning packages to corporate clients in a way that is particularly attractive to global or multinational organizations.

Deutsche Bank, a current client of Duke CE, offers a good illustration of the underlying approach. A senior executive at the bank will identify a series of related problems or business challenges. Some twenty or thirty staff drawn from different countries are selected to work on this problem or challenge. They are divided into groups of about a half dozen individuals. The first stage is for each group to meet, either at the Fuqua campus or at another conference center somewhere else in the world, and spend five (or fewer) days together receiving classroom input (Place). The individuals then return to their jobs and, typically over the next six weeks, consider the problem or challenge using facilitated collaborative working in a virtual community (Space). This is often followed by another classroom (Place) session, followed by another moderated virtual working (Space) component, possibly ending with a final classroom session.

The ratio of Place to Space activities depends on each client's own situation. The bulk of Duke CE's clients are large, global organizations, although there are some U.S.-based clients. For many of these clients, the strategy is to try to integrate learning into work and to do it in such a way that participants are not dependent solely on faculty as the source of knowledge and information but, rather, for them to build their own solutions guided by faculty. Costs will depend on the faculty used and the types of IT setup necessary to put the program into place.

The delivery of different learning experiences depends on building communities within client companies and a cohort within a particular program. As can be seen, the bulk of work is directed around cohorts or teams, although occasionally Duke CE works with senior individuals who require coaching. This means that the company's existing cultural backdrop surrounding the teams is a crucial consideration in designing learning programs. Because the emphasis is on building communities, the types of learning communities already in place—both formal and informal—must be considered.

Participants generally use a combination of bulletin boards to post contributions to problems, real-time or asynchronous sessions, and occasionally CD-ROMs when the organization's technology is not able to fully support online delivery. E-facilitators direct discussion but also try to "bring light, warmth, and structure" to the learning experience: E-learning often runs the risk of being a lonely experience. Further, ways of communicating online are less intuitive than communicating face-to-face, where mood and meaning are more easily ascertained. Building trust before the Space component of the learning begins is essential. Preceding Space with Place (that is, a face-to-face learning event) is seen as a way to build trust and enthusiasm. Participants are often uncomfortable at first with virtual working; because Space does not have a sense of geography or schedule, a culture change within the work environment is often necessary to avoid virtual learning being seen as constantly interruptible.

Implementation Issues
The delivery of a learning opportunity to an audience across the globe using Place and Space represents a considerable departure

from the traditional business school model. A number of organizational and practical issues need to be overcome for this new approach to be effective. Some of these were addressed by the creation of Duke CE as a separate entity, which made it easier to draw on the services of a wider faculty including staff from other business schools, consultants, and people employed by corporate organizations.

When it was first formed, Duke CE employed twenty-four people; at the time of writing, it employed ninety plus an extensive faculty network based around the world. This network includes people responsible for the development of the technology platform, multimedia specialists, and learning designers.

Given the approach, delivery of the learning evidently requires the services of subject matter experts, but, in addition, a new breed of learning facilitator is emerging. According to Ray Smith (director of e-Learning Solutions at Duke CE), this can only be effectively undertaken by people who have given considerable attention to and gained a good awareness of the learning process in its organizational context. A skill shift is also evident in content delivery. Effective classroom delivery, often relying on a charismatic teacher projecting visible enthusiasm and encouraging social interaction, does not necessarily translate to effective delivery using Space. A relatively introverted educator, who may be uncomfortable in the classroom, can often shine in the Space environment. Thus, a wider range of faculty can be employed within a Place and Space environment than might be the case in a traditional setting. New opportunities are emerging.

One important issue, which is a recurring theme in this book, is the ability to deliver programs across different cultures. Here Smith is sanguine, seeing advantages in the Space approach:

> We work in the English language. In the classroom environment, many overseas students do not have sufficient confidence in the English language to feel comfortable in participating. In the Space environment, they have more time to prepare and can be more considered in their input. Further, many students from East Asia

feel a need to be a lot more respectful of the instructor in a classroom than they do when they are typing input to a virtual discussion. Space is a more democratic environment where all voices are equally loud.

Future Developments

Customized programs using Place and Space offer an option for the global client. This is an expanding and profitable business, and Duke CE needs to consider carefully how it can protect what it regards as a leading position in the market.

In the past, this advantage has reflected an early commitment to the effective development of technology. Smith argues that, from the outset when the approach was used on the Global MBA, emphasis was placed on communities of learners learning from each other. E-learning was seen as much more than digitizing content, although high-quality content from subject matter specialists is clearly an essential element in the package. Duke CE is continuing to develop the sophistication of its technology platform. The next generation will extend the capability for synchronous conferencing and allow greater use of video. According to Smith, the use of video will be more "provocative" than concept supportive in its role within learning. In other words, it will inspire a dialogue and develop insights among learners rather than back up a point.

The market for corporate executive education will drive other developments. Duke CE is considering ways in which it can extend the scale of its products and approach. This would enable Duke CE to serve groups of learners numbering in the thousands rather than thirty to forty at a time—which could make corporate change programs considerably more attractive. Another set of opportunities comes from licensing the Place and Space product to other organizations and training them how use it, which would include business schools and training consultancies as well as large corporate organizations. Such "productization," it is believed, could gain additional commercial returns from what Duke CE regards as a well-developed and attractive approach to the delivery of e-learning using a blended technique.

Author's Note: My thanks to Ray Smith of Duke CE for his assistance with this case study.

CAP GEMINI ERNST & YOUNG VIRTUAL BUSINESS SCHOOL

Cap Gemini Ernst & Young UK Ltd was created in May 2000 from the merger of the former management consultancy practice of Ernst & Young with Cap Gemini and Gemini Consulting. The new organization has an impressive list of clients and provides management and solutions consultancy across all sectors of industry, including energy, finance, technology, manufacturing, transport, and government services.

Cap Gemini Ernst & Young (CGEY) employs about 1,000 consulting and support staff in the United Kingdom. The majority of these staff are based in the London head office, although many of the consultants work at client sites for lengthy periods of time.

The Virtual Business School (VBS) was launched in October 1998 by Ernst & Young's management consultancy and, as quoted in an internal e-paper, was seen at the time as: "a way of providing consultants with a range of innovative learning experiences which would address significant gaps in their development, as well as providing a framework within which management consultancy services could create rich and valuable knowledge."

The concept of the VBS emerged out of three broad objectives:

♦ To introduce a greater knowledge/content dimension into learning within the management consultancy practice (building on and complementing the technical, methodological, and personal development programs that already existed)
♦ To provide consultants with a new and different learning opportunity to give them a sense that the company was a place

where access to sources of learning and knowledge exist to enhance their own capabilities

♦ To create a corporate university that was more than simply "rebadging" the training department (a common criticism of the corporate university movement), and in doing so, to make a public demonstration of the company's commitment to the quality and innovativeness of learning and development within CGEY relative to other professional service firms

To create a working VBS, an alliance was formed with Henley Management College. Henley was chosen out of eight short-listed business schools because it was seen to be flexible in its approach and because of its commitment to and understanding of the VBS concept. Indeed, a common vision was apparent between the two entities. These concerned changing the face of business education through business–to–business school connectivity, leading ultimately to the blurring of the physical boundaries among different universities and the creation of a new system of learning providers.

The VBS Centers

Because of the "virtual" nature of the VBS, its form and substance will evolve to reflect the needs of the individual as well as those of the business. The VBS currently has four virtual centers that act as a focus and an operating framework. Typically, each center develops learning programs, events, and activities that:

♦ Are demand led and respond to learning needs
♦ Have a specific knowledge-creation dimension, such as a specific piece of research
♦ Are extended programs of education and development leading to the award of a qualification, such as an M.B.A.

The work of the VBS centers is ultimately to:

♦ Develop and offer accredited and relevant educational programs within the company leading to, for example, M.B.A.s and doctorates
♦ Exploit leading-edge remote-learning technologies, such as "connected classrooms" and training via the Internet

◆ Open a gateway to the wider business school, learning, and knowledge-rich communities
◆ Provide forums where insights and ideas can be shared and developed between staff members from the company and Henley faculty staff, in some cases leading to joint research projects, publications, and/or conferences

The following "centers" were constructed to allow a platform for learning to be established.

1. *The center for postgraduate learning.* This center develops a range of education programs that will lead to the award of a recognized external qualification. These may include a doctoral program and a master's degree in consulting. At present, some sixteen CGEY staff are studying for the MBA. This is viewed as a "challenging program which requires considerable personal investment in terms of time, money and effort."

2. *The center for leadership development.* This center is seen as an informal and indirect means of learning. It concerns itself with "developing learning solutions which increase the leadership capability of the company." The main purpose of the center is to develop learning solutions that increase leadership profile, capability, and performance. Approximately every six weeks, staff members attend a seminar. These sessions are demand led by the business and focus on relevant topics (either technically or of general relevance), such as emotional intelligence and corporate stories.

3. *The center for research and innovation.* This is seen as possibly the most powerful center and often generates outside interest. It can be said that this center is influenced greatly by corporate culture and is ultimately driven by client and business needs. Staff members are given the opportunity to undertake applied research projects (by means of MBA assignments, doctoral theses, joint research papers, and published articles). In addition, in some cases, sponsorship is given by the company for other individuals to undertake research on its behalf. By using applied research methods, intellectual capital is increased and value given to the business by means of the enhancement of thought leadership.

4. *The center for connected learning.* This was initially set up as a

discussion site consisting of forums where individuals could share knowledge. The resource investment for this center was initially very low because it was dependent on the knowledge of forum members. However, this center has developed into a powerful site of connected learning. This center is not viewed as a stand-alone center but as part of an infrastructure capable of supporting other types of centers. A pilot has been created as a virtual business simulation game whereby virtual teams are created that can be cross-cultural or from different offices. These teams are required to operate as a "virtual" business facing the same type of issue, as in reality. This pilot produced positive results, and the center is seen to be capable of supporting strategy and cross-cultural virtual team working.

Challenges for the Future

Challenges facing the VBS concern the degree of connectivity of the organization, management of the centers, and motivation of staff. If expansion of the VBS is to be fruitful, it must be easily accessed by staff members.

Motivation of staff is a key challenge, but this applies to all other forms of learning. Staff members must see value being added to the organization and accept this form of learning technology if it is to be successful. Management of the VBS is also central to its success. Discussion groups will need moderating. This issue has been highlighted in a working paper from Henley Management College.

However, the greatest challenge facing the VBS is the issue of content. How is it possible to tailor the content to individual needs? E-learning is more effective for disseminating technical information. Using e-learning for skills such as influencing is more difficult unless interactivity is promoted to increase self-awareness among participants.

Generally, the key to the future success of the VBS is the exploitation of all available technology to create a fully connected learning center.

GLOBECON

The Globecon Group delivers training on sophisticated financial products and client relationships to the wholesale operations of banks around the world. This is a highly specialized area. Throughout its history, Globecon has concentrated on customized in-house training based on its awareness of product development and the opportunities that it creates for competitive advantage. Inevitably, the precise training curriculum has changed rapidly as global financial markets develop and new instruments emerge.

Globecon was established in 1980 by three specialists who were working for the Chase Manhattan Bank and were delivering programs and consulting services for the bank's corporate clients. Recognizing a market opportunity, the founder members went independent with an initial focus on delivering consultancy workshops to the corporate clients. Over time the workshops proved increasingly attractive to wholesale banks. Their employees needed the knowledge and expertise to sell an increasingly complex range of products to corporate organizations.

Today the Globecon Group has enjoyed consultancy relationships with most of the top financial institutions throughout the world. Clients include Royal Bank of Scotland, Deutsche Bank, Royal Bank of Canada, National Australia Bank, Bank of America, and First Union. Training and consultancy covers a wide range and includes credit, corporate finance, risk management, corporate restructuring, derivatives, and relationship management (the softer interpersonal skills involved in developing and maintaining the client relationship). Based in New York, Globecon employs twenty-five full-time staff and can call on the services of an additional twelve associates.

The Delivery Model

Given the subject area, Globecon training is information or content rich. It is customized to the particular client's needs, and except in the early days, no public or open programs have been offered. The core method of delivery is to hold a series of workshops. A workshop lasts three days and typically five of these workshops (fifteen days total) would be held over an eighteen-month period for up to twenty-five participants. These workshops are supported by preparatory material and reinforced by postcourse material. This material is regarded as essential to the effectiveness of the workshops and is a critical part of the service. In Globecon's view, "Course time should be about application not about acquiring a basic understanding of financial products."

The preparatory and postcourse information was initially produced in the form of paper-based self-instructional packages. Over time "Foundations of Finance" (the preparatory material) and "Finance Update" (the postcourse reinforcement and updating material) became products in their own right. By the mid-1990s, about half of Globecon's revenues came from courses and half from subscriptions for the instructional package. Globecon was, however, anxious to maintain the link between packages and course and reluctant to accept "material only" arrangements with clients.

Given the information-rich nature of Globecon's products, and the wide geographical spread of staff employed by its clients, it is appropriate to ask why Globecon regards the instructor-led workshop as essential.

Gerry Kramer, Globecon's founder and chief executive, argues that the workshop will remain the central element in its training programs:

> You can only carry self-education so far. The reality is that people need interaction with other people. Our course participants do not like to sit in front of a computer for learning, however engaging and clever the technology. Moreover, the value added comes from the ideas generated through interaction in the classroom: This is where the solutions that can be offered to clients are found. You can deliver the analytics without this interaction, but this only takes you to the first stage. After a point it is the qualitative interpretation of the analytics that will produce the gain.

The Impact of the Internet
With this firm commitment to this mixed mode of delivery (which anticipated the now fashionable term *blended learning*; see Chapter 4), it was important that Globecon kept improving abreast of the opportunities afforded by technology. In the mid-1990s, the Group considered using CD-ROMs as a vehicle for distribution. Exploratory investigations, however, revealed that the potential users in wholesale banks did not necessarily have the technology available for access. This channel was rejected and an Internet strategy formulated in 1997.

This strategy did not involve a reformulation of the underlying business model; rather, it extended the existing approach. The difference was that this content would be in an electronic rather than a paper-based format, with its attendant advantages in terms of ease of updating and distribution.

A separate branding for this aspect of the business was created in 1999, and "Fintranet" was launched in 2000. To quote from Globecon's brochure, Fintranet users "automatically receive new cases, deal structures, competency models, assessments, self-study courses, etc., as they are developed." For the user an additional advantage is access at any time, which is supported by a round-the-clock help desk and e-mail facility. This e-mail facility deals with technical product-specific questions as well as access issues.

The Internet facility was developed in conjunction with a software house/specialized IT firm, and it is now maintained by Globecon. Clients are offered access on two bases. If the client wishes to involve more than 130 trainees, a separate dedicated service can be installed that allows greater customization of product. For fewer than that number of trainees (but more than ten), access is directly to Globecon's host system without the intermediary of a dedicated server. Either way the information is held by Globecon, which acts as an ASP. New materials are replicated to the system each week, including timely information regarding deals and structures prevailing in the current marketplace. Globecon's aim is to provide institutions with a total learning system for individual use at an affordable cost. Currently, that translates into per-person annual user charges as low as $300 for access to the entire system.

Updating and distribution via this method has other advantages for client and trainee. The system allows easy tracking and monitoring of participation and reporting on usage for the client wholesale bank. A just-in-time search facility has been introduced to allow immediate knowledge updating for the trainee.

The Future

Globecon has taken what it regarded as the steps necessary to protect and extend its business model. The biggest problem, according to Kramer, has been to secure the finances necessary to develop the systems. The investment has been substantial— almost $6,000,000—not including the twenty-year investment in content.

This will be an ongoing problem. Globecon sees consolidation as inevitable as firms seek partners and mergers to acquire the critical means necessary to sustain the investment. "At present there are too many players in financial education chasing the same clients." The winning consortiums will be those with quality, content, top-of-the-line integrated technology, and the flexibility to supply appropriately customized products to clients.

Globecon retains confidence in its learning or delivery model. In its view, much of the early shine of e-learning has disappeared as the acceptability of online learning becomes questioned and adoption rates are recognized as a problem. In Kramer's view, maintaining learner motivation will become an increasingly important area of concern, and at present, he sees e-learning as offering only partial solutions.

Author's Note: My thanks to Gerry Kramer for his assistance in the preparation of this case study.

CCC/THE MENTORING GROUP

The Mentoring Group is a division of the not-for-profit corporation the Coalition of Counseling Centers (CCC). The CCC was founded in the San Francisco Bay area in 1980 with the intention of providing high-quality, low-cost counseling for individuals, couples, families, and organizations. Much of the early activity was conducted through churches and donated after-hours at physicians' offices.

The scope of the services developed and the group expanded into consulting, training, and publishing. The Mentoring Group was formally established in 1997 as a division of CCC. By 2001, six part-time consultants; four part-time support staff; and an extended network of suppliers, IT specialists, and sympathetic organizations and individuals were involved in the delivery of The Mentoring Group's products and services. Corporate clients include some well-known names: Lucent Technologies, Microsoft Corporation, Conoco, and PricewaterhouseCoopers. The Group has been particularly associated with the mentoring programs introduced at Hewlett-Packard, and this aspect of its work is considered in the case study in Chapter 2.

Notwithstanding the expansion, The Mentoring Group is firmly committed to mentoring as its core products and activity. It defines mentoring as "the process in which successful individuals go out of their way to help others establish goals and develop skills to reach them." The skills, knowledge, and attitudes acquired by the mentee enhance performance and satisfaction inside and outside the workplace; the Group sees its work as socially important and worthwhile and has a commitment to mentoring that extends beyond business success.

Mentoring is an activity that requires the recognition and development of a range of soft, interpersonal skills. The growing availability of technology as a distribution and delivery channel has, however, had an important effect on the way that The Mentoring Group delivers its service to clients.

Developments Before the Internet

At an early stage, The Mentoring Group realized the potential value of technology as a means of distributing its products and services to a wider audience. Much of the initial work took place in collaboration with Hewlett-Packard in the early 1990s, before the wider emergence of the Internet. The approach developed involved in-person workshops and then the use of telephone-based audioconferencing and role-play sessions. All participants received a full PowerPoint pack of training slides in advance of the training session along with printed study materials. Participants were asked to skim the materials in advance, do a prestudy exercise, and open the slides on their computers at the time of the live training. The session would then proceed with the opportunity for questioning, discussion, and role-play practice.

The Mentoring Group was therefore prepared for the impact of the Internet. Its underlying strategy is to see improvements in technology (including the Internet itself) as a continuum that allows it to deliver training in mentoring more effectively.

The Web Site

For a consultancy organization that focuses on soft-skills training, The Mentoring Group was an early mover and established a Web site in January 1998. From the outset, however, a firm decision was made that the site should contain far more than information and advertising on the Group's products and services. The ambitious aim was "to bring the concept and importance of mentoring as an activity to the widest possible audience"; the approach has been exploratory, and the role of the site in the Group's activity has developed and will continue to do so.

As well as details of the Group's commercial products and services, in its current form, the site *(www.mentoringgroup.com)* contains two important free services. The first consists of a range of ideas and tips for both mentors and mentees. There is also an archive of relevant articles and commentaries available that can be freely downloaded from the site. For example, the Group makes available several tools for creating a vision and a development plan for working with a mentor.

The second facility is an easy link to an e-mail help line. Every serious inquiry on a mentoring topic e-mailed through the Group's site will receive a reply without any charge being incurred by the inquirer. Many of these questions can receive a standard reply, but the resource commitment is considerable. Some 250 e-mails will be received in any given month. Without question, the main motivation for the Group's Internet policy stems from its commitment to make mentoring more widely understood and practiced. Staff do, however, recognize that it has brought them associated commercial advantages. A respected and effective Web site is essential in protecting the core business. In July 2001, the site received its one millionth hit; The Mentoring Group will appear high on the listing of any search engine where "mentoring" is entered.

Some important questions arise, since given the existing state of tracking information (clickstream data), the Group has little information on who the site's visitors were, their motivation in accessing the site, how they used the material, and the benefit they obtained as a result. Vicki Bahnsen, The Mentoring Group's administrative manager and training coordinator, says the need for better quality information is an issue, but one that is unlikely to be solved in the short term. Her main current problems concern the need to maintain the freshness of the site by updating contents monthly and the difficulties of delivery to a multitude of clients across different technological infrastructures. Eventually, the Group would like to deliver live training on a regular basis and add a chat room to the site's facilities, but it is not yet ready to implement these options effectively.

Mentoring and the Internet
The Group has consciously considered the role that the Internet should play as a delivery channel in its business strategy and in the achievement of its wider social objectives. All training consultants who specialize in soft skills, however, face a fundamental question: Will the face-to-face interaction always be required and will technology eventually make the trainer superfluous? Linda Phillips-Jones, who was a founding member and has been with the Group since 1980, is clear in her response:

Whatever the technology enables, however much audioconferencing develops, it will always be best if a skilled trainer observes learners' performance and gives them feedback. Now we recommend that a local expert be physically present observing learners at each site. In the future, the expert could provide online skill demonstrations and carefully monitor performance through precise, easy-to-use, inexpensive Web-cams and very careful listening.

Given this view, and the Group's commitment to ethical standards, it is likely that a number of problems could arise in the area of managing and monitoring at a distance. A good illustration is offered when the Group undertakes global programs for which an additional dimension of difficulties is present because of different cultural approaches.

To date, the Group has delivered computer-based and audioconference programs in the Asia Pacific region and Europe as well as the United States and Canada. Also at present, The Mentoring Group staff are not bilingual. Therefore, different degrees of ability in the English language make the maintenance of the pace of programs difficult. However, in Phillips-Jones's view, a subtler problem concerns what she describes as the "silence pause." Given the cultural differences between, for example, Australia and Malaysia, how is silence to be interpreted by a facilitator based in California who is running a program with fifteen participants in the Asia Pacific region? Current interventions that can ameliorate such difficulties include using cofacilitators/performance observers in host countries, sending more preparatory material in advance of the session, calling on quiet participants (while avoiding embarrassing anyone), and using more chat facilities. This whole area of "distance management" remains a topic of significant concern, and The Mentoring Group is determined not to solve (or avoid) it by offering lightweight versions of its products and services.

Author's Note: My thanks to Linda Phillips-Jones and Vicki Bahnsen for their assistance in the preparation of this case study.

LEARNSHARE

In 1996, training managers at General Motors, 3M, Motorola, Owens Corning, Deere & Co., Eaton, Pilkington, Owens-Illinois, Northwest Airlines, Pfizer Inc., Chevron, Levi Strauss & Co., and Verizon realized that by working together their organizations could save money on training and benefit from a collective expertise by sharing the products they developed within their own organizations.

The training managers realized that the selling of technology-enabled training was packaged to meet vendors' needs. The terms of licenses, the costs of multimedia training, and the requirement to commit to high-volume purchases did not meet their companies' needs.

In addition, there was a feeling that quality was not all that it might be; too much material was overly text based and lacking in stimulation. Around this time, new suppliers were entering the market, often with better-quality products, although there were still substantial gaps. In addition, the thirteen founder companies themselves were producing learning materials, but in-house production of quality materials was expensive and time-consuming.

The training managers responded by establishing LearnShare as a consortium to pool the resources and knowledge of these thirteen noncompeting corporations. Its shared mission is to:

♦ Provide a market space with best-in-class learning products and services, including a portal to carefully selected learning resources, and easy access to world-class strategic partners
♦ Facilitate benchmarking and sharing of best practices that capitalizes on the experience and expertise of industry leaders
♦ Leverage the collective strength of collaborating companies in evaluating and acquiring products
♦ Provide specialized services that build customized solutions for unique needs

♦ Act as a first-level clearinghouse for vendor and provider selection

Half a million courses are now available through LearnShare. As well as the thirteen charter member companies, for an annual fee of $50,000 (which is about half the cost of a training manager) companies can join as subscribers. With the recent addition of new subscribers CNA, United Parcel Service, and AT&T Broadband, the LearnShare network now encompasses more than 2.5 million employees.

The LearnShare Model

Until recently, LearnShare members were required to cooperate by sharing courses that they have developed themselves. Thus, an accounting course developed for General Motors might be used in Levi Strauss, or Owens Corning could use a sales course put together by 3M. Member companies can amend, amalgamate, and generally adapt such shared courses to their own use, with their own logos and house branding, but usually there will also be an acknowledgment to LearnShare.

LearnShare encountered some problematic issues in sharing existing content. Not all organizations are created equally. Some members devoted a substantial effort to authoring and producing many original programs while others opted to work with outside vendors that retained the rights to the programs. Other organizations developed personality-dependent programs, that is, instructor-led programs built and delivered by one person. These personality-based programs were typically dynamic in execution but light on documentation, making it difficult for anyone outside of the author to present the program. Despite these challenges, LearnShare's thirteen founders contributed close to 100 original programs to the consortium pool—programs that were then used by other members as is, to create derivative works, and by the consortium as a whole to develop Web-based programs.

LearnShare is able to use its resulting market power by seeking the best in class and negotiating best prices with third-party vendors. Then, rather than being forced to purchase a license for a specific number of programs and a limited audience, courses are available on a pay-per-use basis so that member companies can determine whether they suit their needs before making a large financial commitment. If the courses do suit, they will subsequently purchase them. This not only benefits member companies but vendors, because it helps them come to market and test products more quickly.

In a sense, LearnShare could be said to act as the e-learning department of member companies. It has four full-time staff, with a chief executive who is seconded from one of the member companies on a two-year basis. Additionally, it is supported by contractors on a project basis and expert groups made up of representatives from member companies, who advise on technology and learning methodologies and test courses. LearnShare is also developing the ability to map competencies in member companies, leading to the appropriate development of new products. Its Web site is becoming increasingly robust and can now register students, track usage, and operate billing systems.

Focus of Activities

LearnShare claims that members and subscribers benefit from their involvement through improved cycle time, decreased cost, more focused experimentation, and an increase in learning and development that supports the bottom line: "Sixteen companies can achieve collectively what one can't," says Lois Webster, general manager. "Being a member/subscriber of LearnShare accelerates a company's productivity and increases their access to creative solutions. In addition, large companies make substantial savings through cost avoidance and small companies launch more quickly into the e-learning world."

LearnShare works to integrate its Web site with each company's unique technology infrastructure. If the company needs a learning management system to offer and track courses, the LearnShare Web site is capable of providing these services. For companies that have learning management systems already in place, LearnShare integrates their e-learning component seamlessly with their technology.

LearnShare is increasingly finding that it has the ability to influence providers of learning materials. More and more it is looking for products that make the best use of media, and those that are most captivating. LearnShare started mainly by providing courses in softer skills, such as leadership, sales, and customer relations, because these were not company or sector specific and were suitable for collaboration. Now it is moving into the provision of courses in IT, finance, compliance, and health and safety.

Delivery channels have changed over time. Over a three-year period, LearnShare has moved from providing 85 percent of its material in the form of text-based CD-ROMs to making 85 percent of material available over the Web (and this material is much less text based).

As organizations provide and require more Web-based learning and development opportunities for their employees, members are able to experiment with the products in the low-risk environment provided by LearnShare. One emerging trend that members have tested is a move from the classroom to a blended approach, which includes part e-learning and part classroom learning. Another trend is the increase in the use of synchronous communication between students and facilitators in the e-learning environment. The onus is increasingly being placed on the students to develop the necessary skills, and to become independent, self-sufficient learners. LearnShare is giving learners the environment and the tools they need.

LearnShare is now working consultatively with each member/subscriber company to develop an e-learning strategy that addresses business objectives, carefully targets a learning road map for key audiences, selects the best Web-based courses to augment the company's training program, and customizes the Web site to integrate with internal technology infrastructure.

The Future
LearnShare expects the trends of the past few years—greater connectivity, livelier, more interesting products—to continue. Although LearnShare is already available globally, it is currently de-

veloping more tools in this direction. LearnShare's vendor information system is being designed to provide members with substantive vendor profiles that will make the process of identifying vendors that are capable of global delivery easier. Also, LearnShare works with its suppliers, to communicate the need for materials in languages other than English and in forms that suit other cultures. It continually links the needs to the resources.

LearnShare also facilitates the sharing of best practices through on-site and virtual seminars. Recent seminar topics included best practices in e-learning, launching a corporate university, and the return on investment for the corporate training dollar. LearnShare invites industry experts to present current issues and trends and members to share best-practice experiences on the topics.

LearnShare is also considering expanding its activities through franchising. Possible targets include countries outside the United States, and other industry areas such as the public sector or small businesses, which are currently unable to afford e-learning products.

Author's Note: My thanks to Lois Webster, general manager of LearnShare, for her assistance in the preparation of this case study.

Chapter 8

Trainers and the New Economy

"When you come to a fork in the road, take it."

The previous chapter considered the effect that the new economic environment will have on the training industry. In this chapter, some wider social issues are discussed. At their heart is a beguilingly simple question: Are the new opportunities for improved training a good thing for society?

The market for training will become more efficient.

A straightforward, uncritical, positive response should be resisted. There are a number of implications to be considered. It is unquestionably true that, in common with everything that the Internet affects, the market for training will become more efficient. It is equally true that the balance of power will shift to the consumer—the learner who is the user of training. However, there are some important social issues to be considered on the distribution of access to training opportunities. This raises the question, should HR professionals seek to take an active position on the social issues or remain passive players merely responding to the changing forces that influence the training market?

These questions are the subject of this chapter. The underlying point is Proposition 20.

―――――― **Proposition 20** ――――――

Social inclusion is emerging as a key political issue. Trainers have the power to influence the debate positively.

It is hard to gainsay the argument that the issue of social inclusion is a legitimate concern for government. What is less certain is what it may or may not have to do with trainers—except in their capacity as individual citizens.

The premise underlying this chapter is that social inclusion should be of concern. Trainers should be concerned about the issue, and with the arrival of the connected economy, the trainer has a unique opportunity to make a positive contribution.

Inclusion, Access, and Distribution

In its report on the future of training technology, the ASTD included the following observation from the American novelist William Gibson: "The future's already arrived—it's just not evenly distributed yet."[1]

Certainly the better examples of the application of e-learning described in the case studies in this book could be said to offer a glimpse of the future for some individuals in some organizations. However, there are many issues to be considered before concluding that e-learning for all is a universal panacea.

E-learning has the potential to bring enormous benefits to a great number of individuals. This is true of all applications of the Internet. However, as with any significant economic change, there is a change in the balance of power. Some organizations and individuals gain at the expense of others.

Divisions based on technology could prove more intractable than the ideological divisions of the cold war.

There is a whole range of potentially disadvantaged groups whose position should be recognized. Far and away the most important issue is international disparities surrounding access to technology. Jeffrey Sachs, Harvard professor of international trade, writing in the

Economist presents a powerful case for this proposition. He argues that divisions based on technology could prove more intractable than the ideological divisions of the cold war:

> A small part of the globe, accounting for some 15% of the Earth's population, provides nearly all of the world's technology innovations. A second, involving perhaps half of the world's population, is able to adopt these technologies in production and consumption. The remaining part, covering around a third of the world's population, is technology-disconnected, neither innovating at home nor adopting foreign technologies.[2]

Professor Sachs argues that unless action is taken, the divisions will become greater: Regions with the advanced technologies are best placed to innovate further and have access to larger markets. He suggests that three things need to happen:

> First, the new technology-driven character of the global economy must be thought through: Geography, public health and ecology must be brought into the analysis of technological change and economic growth. Second, governments need to change their approach to aid, spending more and more wisely. Third, participation in informational assistance needs to be broadened and recast. Multinational firms and First-World universities and scientific establishments need to be engaged, and the official agencies charged with global development (the IMF, the World Bank, and the various UN agencies) must be reformed.[3]

This is a demanding agenda, but the problem is critical. Action is needed if the 2 billion people who live in these technologically disconnected regions are to benefit from globalization.

Domestic problems in the developed countries surrounding inclusion, access, and distribution pale by comparison. However, if WBT does develop as expected, it is possible to identify three potential categories of the "e-learning disconnected":

1. People who, by virtue of the nature of their employment (or non-employment), will not get access to training opportunities and self-development through e-learning
2. People who are computer-phobic
3. Organizations that are not, and will not be, at the leading edge because they do not have the ability to invest in the technology

All three of these categories could properly be seen as the concern of government. However, a brief comment should be offered on the third point. Although there is some truth in the suggestion that there may be e-learning-disconnected organizations, this should not be a focus of significant concern. This view is offered for the following reasons, which reflect many of the arguments developed throughout this book. First, there will be few organizations that will manage without an effective technology platform of some kind. Second, the demand for e-learning will lead to the emergence of vendors or suppliers that will offer suitable products or solutions for smaller organizations. Third, as the stream of case studies throughout this book has demonstrated, the case for adopting the all-powerful e-learning system is still to be proven. For some organizations, it may be appropriate to invest in such a system; for others the case will be far from self-evident. The market will develop and change. The more appropriate focus for concern should be the disadvantaged individual.

Access and Inclusion: A Policy Response

In 2000, the ASTD and the National Governors Association (NGA) convened a Commission on Technology and Adult Learning. Its mission was ambitious: to define and encourage a technology-enabled learning environment that will result in an engaged citizenry and a skilled workforce for the digital economy.

In June the following year, a report entitled "A Vision of E-Learning for America's Workforce" was published.[4] The report summarized the current position on the development of e-learning in the United States and anticipated exciting and inevitable developments: "a future in which e-learning allows learning to become a continuous process of inquiry and improvement that keeps pace with the speed of change in business and society.[5]

The report recommends or encourages government and business to play a leadership role in overcoming the issues of access. The challenge and opportunity were seen as realizing "e-learning's potential for reducing the divide between the 'haves' and the 'have nots' " in America today. E-learning was seen as having the potential to address some critical social issues. These included growing economic disparities between sections of the population, which could be narrowed by broadening access to high-quality education and training. E-learning could assist in overcoming low levels of literacy. In short, while it is not a panacea, "e-learning can help to strengthen democracy and community by broadening access to the information people need to improve their lives and the lives of those around them."[6]

This full potential would, however, only be realized if effective structures were in place. A policy debate and some interventions are required since "by acting together now, government, business and education have the opportunity to shape America's e-learning future."[7]

The commission established by the ASTD and NGA identified and reported on three critical issues. These were, first, quality (create the highest-quality e-learning experiences possible); second, assessment and certification (implement new measures for assessing and certifying what individuals know and are able to do); and, third, access (ensure broad and equitable access to e-learning opportunities). Each of these areas was considered in turn and a series of recommendations advanced. Those concerned with access, which is the main focus of this part of the book, are set out in Focus Point 31.

One example cited in the ASTD/NGA report was Michigan Virtual University. Because this provides an illustration of an organization rising to the new challenges, it forms the case study at the end of this chapter.

Focus Point 31: Recommendations for E-Learning Access

♦ Adopt common technical standards aimed at promoting open and equitable access while reducing development costs.
♦ Create conditions that favor e-learning and eliminate barriers that inhibit people from engaging in e-learning.
♦ Provide incentives and foster public/private partnerships to promote broader access to e-learning among underserved communities.
♦ Provide leadership in demonstrating the power of e-learning for individuals and communities.
♦ Use the "bully pulpit" to speak out on behalf of e-learning.

A Professional Response: Open Source

At the start of this chapter, it was suggested that with the arrival of the connected economy, the training profession has a unique opportunity to make a positive contribution to issues on inclusion. In fact, the challenge facing the training profession is much broader. Encouraging greater inclusion is one of a series of issues facing the profession; another is the case for cooperation.

Arguments concerning professional cooperation are complex. They concern the extent to which a group should seek to act as a group to make its products or skills more widely available as a matter of principle. An apt illustration may prove more helpful than a philosophical discussion at this stage. An illustration is drawn from IT, particularly the writing of Tim Berners-Lee and the open-source movement.

As noted in Chapter 1, Berners-Lee worked at CERN, the European Organization for Nuclear Research (the subject of a case study included in Chapter 4). In the early 1990s, he designed the basic software infrastructure for communication that led to the Internet: He has been justifiably described as the Internet's inventor. In 1999, he co-wrote a book entitled *Weaving the Web*. His book is of interest for two reasons: first, because of the historical account of the development of the Internet; and, second, because much of the book deals with his belief that openness of standards and of access is the appropriate way forward for the Web.

Berners-Lee's idealism shines through his book:

> My original vision for a universal Web was an armchair aid to help people do things in the web of real life. It would be a mirror, reflecting reports or conversations or art and mapping social interactions. But more and more, the mirror model is wrong, because interaction is taking place primarily on the Web. People are using the Web to build things they have not built or written or drawn or communicated anywhere else. As the Web becomes a primary space for much activity, we have to be careful that it allows for a just and fair society. The Web must allow equal access to those in different economic and political situations; those who have physical or cognitive disabilities; those of different cultures; and those who use different languages with different characters that read in different directions across a page.[8]

One practical result of this idealism is that all Web code (the lines of programming) has been open-source software. Anyone can access, use, edit, and rebuild the code. "Open source" has developed into a movement with adherents from the software movement. Its philosophy is of interest at this stage of the book.

Open source is basically software developed by uncoordinated but collaborating programmers, using freely distributed source and the communications of the Internet. The open-source movement consists of individuals who believe that open-source development creates better software than can be developed in a corporate or proprietary environment.

The very nature of the open-source movement means that it is hard to identify a simple, cohesive strand. On the other hand, not unexpectedly, a wealth of information, discussion, and analysis is available on the Web.[9]

Chris DiBona, S. Ockman, and M. Stone, writing an introduction to the open-source movement, begin with a consideration of the circumstances that led to the discovery of the structure of DNA. There was a strong competitive element and some ethical issues over secrecy. James Watson, who together with Francis Crick made the crucial breakthrough, felt uncomfortable with the need for secrecy: He felt that professional competition led to a delay in disclosing information, and the progress of science was affected. DiBona and colleagues summarize:

> Science, after all, is ultimately an Open-Source enterprise. The scientific method rests on the process of discovery, and a process of justification. For scientific results to be justified, they must be replicable. Replication is not possible unless the source is shared: the hypothesis, the test conditions, and the results. The process of discovery can follow many paths, and at times scientific discoveries do occur in isolation. But ultimately the process of discovery must be served by sharing information: enabling other scientists to go forward where one cannot; pollinating the ideas of others so that something new may grow that otherwise would not have been born.[10]

The philosophical approach here can easily be extended to software. To quote from the *opensource.org* Web page:

> The basic idea behind open source is very simple. When programmers on the Internet can read, redistribute and modify the source for a

piece of software, it evolves. People improve it, people adapt it, people fix bugs. And this can happen at a speed that, if one is used to the slow pace of conventional software development, seems astonishing.[11]

We in the open-source community have learned that this rapid evolutionary process produces better software than the traditional closed model, in which only a very few programmers can see source and everybody else must blindly use an opaque block of bits.

Open-source development creates better software than can be developed in a corporate or proprietary environment.

Shared development of software, then, is more effective and produces a better end result. Open-source development, runs the argument, creates better software than can be developed in a corporate or proprietary environment. It is more robust and can be better supported and more innovative. This has led to a number of developments to promote initiatives designed to put such beliefs into practice.

The open-source movement has many strands. An underlying issue to be considered is the commercial imperative that must drive many producers of software. If sharing of information is a good thing socially, how could commercial organizations be encouraged to share? In the early stages of the debate, a researcher at MIT, Richard Stallman, advocated an approach based on "free software." This is software for which the developers permit users the freedom to:

♦ Run the program for any purpose.
♦ Study how the program works, and adapt it.
♦ Redistribute copies.
♦ Improve the program, and release improvements so that the whole community benefits.

Access to the source code is necessarily a precondition for use of this software (see *www.gnu.org*).

In 1997, a group of developers met to consider the implications and raise the profile of free software. One key decision was an agreement to use the term *open-source software* rather than *free software*. This term assists by emphasizing the critical underlying distinction: Such software must be nonproprietary (open to distribution and development), not necessarily noncommercial—developers and distributors may charge for their service. Organizations and individuals may, through offering a value-added service, generate income through software that is licensed open source.

The most prominent subsequent development has been the emergence of Linux, an operating system developed initially by Linus Torvalds, a student at the University of Helsinki. Linux has emerged as a significant competitor to Microsoft operating systems. It was developed by a loosely knit group of programmers, is downloaded from the Internet at no charge, and can be distributed and modified. It is licensed under an open-source public license, and companies and developers may charge as long as the open-source principles are observed.[12]

The Professional Agenda for Trainers

The open-source movement is a professional response to the issues raised by inclusion, access, and distribution at a time of disruptive technology. Readers may wish to reflect whether there are analogies between open-source software and training models. Should, for example, the profession seek to develop a set of tools designed to assist individuals to acquire basic skills and make them freely available?

The difficulty here is that the HR profession in general and trainers in particular have been reluctant to take a stance—and such stances have tended not to go beyond "learning is a good thing." This is doubtless one of the attractions of the rather woolly concept of the learning organization that was outlined in Chapter 3. This section concludes with a brief consideration of the actions that professionals could take now. A first suggestion is set out in Proposition 21.

—————————— **Proposition 21** ——————————

More honesty and less hype are required if the training profession is to grasp the new opportunity to maximum effect.

The long-term credibility of the profession may depend on an honest appraisal of successes and failures.

This proposition suggests that propaganda should not drive the debate. There is plenty for trainers to achieve and a great deal of satisfaction to be gained without overstating the potential advantages to be derived from e-learning. More important, the long-term credibility of the profession, at this stage of transition, may depend on an honest appraisal of successes and failures.

At present, much of the emphasis on e-learning is on marketing. Conference organizers are busily promoting events that combine contributions from training managers and industry experts. It is in the corporate training manager's personal and professional interest to give a positive gloss to events. It is obviously more palatable to present a case study as a success. High profile does not, however, necessarily mean successful embedding of product or process. To introduce a lighter note, no one has as yet, as far as I am aware, offered the sort of conference case study parodied in Focus Point 32.

It is evidently in the interests of suppliers or vendors of technology-based learning products to give the best impression of the acceptance of their products. This combined marketing effect from training managers and vendors may detract attention from the need for a hard-edged evaluation of results and shaping of information if e-learning is to be embedded effectively.

If this all seems unduly cynical, consider the following. First, in my experience, the age of CBT and CD-ROMs led to purchase of material that did not find sufficient acceptance by many users and is now littering cupboards the length and breadth of the land. Second, finding case studies for this book proved difficult. On several occasions, training vendors were asked if they could assist by facilitating introductions to training managers who were using their systems. The initial response was invariably helpful and positive; the final result was often a message that, at this stage, it was too early to share any

Focus Point 32: The Conference Paper We Will Never See

Gary Holmes is training manager of Lakin Scott Golding, a firm of 3,000 employees with two manufacturing sites and one headquarters site in Kentucky.

In 1999, as the result of cost pressures, Lakin Scott Golding switched from predominantly classroom training to electronically based training delivered through CBT and later the company intranet. The result was chaos and, in this session, Gary Holmes will describe how:

♦ Incompatibility of IT systems and the chosen products led to huge overruns and how the launch and promotion was delayed three times
♦ A learning cafe was set up and how it rapidly degenerated into a badly maintained spare meeting room
♦ Many of the soft-skill modules available on the system were used once by participants and found to be both trivial in content and difficult to access
♦ A series of uncoordinated interventions emerged in parts of the business where concerned managers sent their staff on unauthorized external courses, with a resulting lack of budgetary control

Holmes, an experienced speaker at conferences, is soon to establish a consultancy specializing in change management.

Author's Note: Gary Holmes and Lakin Scott Golding are purely fictitious, and any resemblance to individuals or organizations is purely coincidental.

information. This makes my gratitude to those who did participate by providing case studies, and for the honesty of their responses, even more profound.

This leads to a specific suggestion. In the course of the research for this book, hard information on time and space to learn proved most elusive. Such information obtained on the new approaches to learning were discussed in Chapter 5. There is evidently a paucity of relevant research to assist the training manager in the age of e-learning. The key questions on how, when, and where individuals prefer to learn were set out in Focus Point 20. In my view, there is an evident need to encourage the creation of repositories where trainers can share their answers and ideas.

Training, Education, and the New Opportunity

To some readers, these discussions on inclusion and on the professional response will seem an irrelevance; to others, it is of considerable importance. To those in the latter group, a final brief incursion may appeal.

This is simply the memorial on the tombstone of an eighteenth-century Norfolk blacksmith who was buried some three miles from where this book was written:

> Johnson Jex / Born in obscurity he passed his days at Letheringsett / A village blacksmith / By the force of an original and inventive genius / Combined with indomitable perseverance / He mastered some of the greatest difficulties of science / Advancing from the forge to the crucible / And from the horse-shoe to the chronometer / Acquiring by mental labour / And philosophic research / A vast and varied amount of mechanical skill / And general knowledge / He was a man of scrupulous integrity / But regardless of wealth / And insensitive to the voice of fame / He lived and died a scientific anchorite / Aged 73

Why is this relevant to the themes of this book? The fact is simply that, for many people, training and education are rather special goods and interventions. The acquisition of job-related skills gives people pride in their work: They can acquire new confidence and self-respect. Johnson Jex achieved his immense accomplishments without e-learning—but what would he have made of the Internet?

There is an ethical dimension to all of this. Much of the motivation that leads me to write this book comes from a childhood in industrial South Wales where schoolteacher values prevailed. These values are about creating and sharing, rather than exploiting new opportunities solely for personal advantage. May e-learning develop in this tradition.

Notes

1 D. Abernathy, H. Allerton, T. Barron, and J. Salopek, "Trendz," *Training and Development,* November 1999, 22–43. I am grateful to Pat Galagan, editor-in-chief of *Training and Development,* for drawing my attention to this quotation.

2 J. Sachs, "Sachs on Globalization: A New Map of the World," *Economist,* June 24, 2000, 113.

3 Ibid.

4 ASTD/NGA Center for Best Practice, "A Vision of E-Learning for America's Workforce." (Alexandria, Va:, ASTD, 2001).

5 Ibid., 4.

6 Ibid., 12.

7 Ibid., 4.

8 T. Berners-Lee with M. Fischetti, *Weaving the Web* (London: Orion Business Books, 1999), 178.

9 On the open-source movement, see *http://release1.edventure.com/index.cfm; www.gnu.org/philosophy;* and *www.opensource.org.*

10 C. DiBona, S. Ockman, and M. Stone, "Introduction," in *Open Sources: Voices from the Open Source Revolution,* ed. C. DiBona and S. Ockman. (Farnham, U.K.: O'Reilly & Associates, 1999). See also *www.oreilly.com/catalog/opensources/book/intro.html.*

11 See *www.opensource.org.*

12 See *www.linux.com.*

MICHIGAN VIRTUAL UNIVERSITY

In 1996, Michigan governor John Engler and a coalition of automakers and universities established the Michigan Virtual Automotive College to pursue means of delivering workforce training electronically. It would become the prototype for the Michigan Virtual University (MVU). Realizing the need to decrease Michigan's heavy dependence on manufacturing industries, state leaders in 1998 launched the Michigan Virtual University to help the state move toward a broader-based knowledge economy.

MVU's value to the people of Michigan is twofold:

♦ First, it is a vehicle through which Michigan's workforce can gain up-to-date skills. In this capacity, MVU serves as an economic development catalyst, since a skilled workforce helps retain and draw new businesses to the state.

♦ Second, MVU has a role in assisting Michigan's schools in the transformation to a technology-based knowledge economy and in stimulating their capacity to provide electronic learning opportunities.

Seeded with a five-year grant from the state's Strategic Fund, MVU is a private, nonprofit organization now moving toward self-sufficiency through sales of products and services and grant-funded projects.

MVU offerings include both credit and noncredit courses. Generally, MVU brokers courses and training modules through the state's colleges, universities, and private training providers. MVU does not independently grant degrees; credentials earned by participants are done so through the organization providing the course or module. MVU does, however, develop a limited number of courses, most often on a contractual basis for specific customers and programs.

Workforce Development

On the commercial side, MVU provides Michigan companies and associations with a variety of options for delivering training to their employees. For smaller companies, MVU may create a company-branded extranet stocked with off-the-shelf courses. In some cases, MVU may customize an existing course to company-specific processes or develop an entirely new curriculum in collaboration with company trainers and subject matter experts. For example, the Automotive College repurposed training content that was proprietary to the Ford Motor Company for Web delivery to Ford's approved suppliers. Today, MVU is working with the Society of Manufacturing Engineers, which has 60,000 members in seventy countries, to repurpose ten of its most popular courses, such as lean manufacturing and cell manufacturing, for Web delivery.

Even on the commercial side, however, MVU fulfills a public policy role that stretches from government agencies to the state's smallest businesses. For example, MVU recently created a blended solution to assist as many as 27,000 health care providers to meet new Medicaid Uniform Billing requirements. The project included an online course, a face-to-face version that could be offered by community colleges, and an online instructor guide. Funded by the Michigan Department of Community Health, the courses are available at no cost to users or the colleges.

Another important initiative launched in early 2002 addresses both training and access issues for Michigan's smallest businesses. With funding from the Michigan Department of Career Development, MVU brokered course content and developed the Business Electronic Education Freeway (*www.beefreeway.org*), a Web site for companies with twenty-five or fewer employees to provide no-cost access to 1,400 minicourses in IT and soft skills. These same courses are available to other businesses, as well, which may purchase any number of them on a volume-priced basis.

Academic Initiatives

Michigan Community College Virtual Learning Collaborative
A key success for MVU is its partnership with the Michigan Community College Association in the Virtual Learning Collaborative (VLC) which unites the state's twenty-eight public community colleges in a virtual system. The VLC has a uniform statewide tuition such that anyone living in a district providing tax support to a community college pays the "in district" rate. Through the VLC, students are admitted to the nearest community college, known as the "home college," and are then able to enroll in online courses at any participating college. The home college provides students with transcripts, test proctoring, and support services. About 13,000 students enrolled in 2000–2001. The courses on offer are a mixture of new courses and traditional courses reconfigured for online delivery.

Professional Development
MVU's professional development programs for faculty and teachers are a growing source of revenue and reputation. In 2000–2001, MVU provided training for more than 275 educators seeking to become online instructors or trainers of new cohorts. MVU is continually developing programs to help educators effectively integrate technology into the curriculum, discovering best practices for teaching online, and developing online courses.

In 2000, the State of Michigan provided 88,000 Michigan K–12 public classroom teachers with a laptop computer or other technology through a program managed by MVU. To participate, teachers were required to submit a self-assessment of their technology skills, providing MVU with what is believed to be the largest such database nationwide. MVU is using the results to develop tracks and workshops that target the skill deficits that the teachers themselves identified.

IT Training Initiative
Under a three-year contract with a private sector training provider, the IT training initiative provides more than 700 minicourses in IT and soft skills free to all students, teachers, faculty, and staff at Michigan nonprofit education institutions. The minicourses may be used, in part or whole, as tutorials or independent courses, or may be incorporated into new courses with wraparounds and/or other content. In addition, under an agreement with the State Board of Education, the minicourses may earn teachers continuing education credits for licensing purposes.

Michigan Virtual High School
Approved by the Michigan legislature in 2000, the Michigan Virtual High School launched a fall 2001 pilot, with full-scale operation set for fall 2002. It offers courses that high schools might not otherwise be able to offer and reaches students who, for a variety of reasons, may be unable to attend classes. All courses are taught by MVU-trained, Michigan-certified high school teachers. Especially successful is the Advanced Placement program, which enables students to earn high school and college credit concurrently. More than 1,200 Advanced Placement and 400 core

course enrollments are expected for the 2001–2002 academic year, with as many as 10,000 students using the free AP Exam Review course and 500 teachers using the Teacher Tools.

Career Development Services
At the behest of the Michigan Department for Career Development, MVU has developed several career guidance programs, including:

- *TalentFreeway.org,* a comprehensive one-stop shop for Michigan employers and job seekers offering free job and résumé postings at a basic level, as well as higher-level, fee-based services
- *MyDreamExplorer.org,* an online system licensed to middle and high schools that enables users (students, teachers, parents, and counselors) to explore careers and map education options toward their interests and goals

Challenges Faced
The staff of the MVU is relatively small, with only about fifty full-time employees. Because of its size, the MVU has had to focus on its key priorities and tries to choose the most efficient and inexpensive ways of achieving these aims. This is one reason that the MVU decided to act as a broker of courses, rather than to develop its own.

Technology
Because MVU has many initiatives running and developing in parallel, different learning management systems have been put into use for different programs. Now, the IT Team faces the challenge of coordinating and integrating them, especially to allow user profiling and a central catalog search function. MVU's system includes a LearnFrame learning management system for IT courses and commercial intranets, a BlackBoard system and database that launches community college and high school courses, and a third proprietary system that hosts noncredit courses and those from four-year education institutions.

Four-Year Degree Programs
Four-year colleges and universities typically operate more independently of each other than do other educational institutions.

Many have sufficient resources to develop their own online programs and limitations on how credits may be transferred between institutions. Consequently, it has become a bigger challenge to get four-year colleges and universities to move their online courses and programs forward through a central access site such as MVU.

Evaluation and Accreditation
Accreditation of courses is an issue that the MVU has not yet fully addressed. Currently, all accreditation rests with the course provider.

MVU's small team of in-house instructional designers has created a course evaluation system that incorporates online teaching principles developed by renowned education leaders with a computer-based tool. MVU-developed courses can be assessed against these evaluation standards, as well as courses procured from education and commercial vendors. The intent is to develop these quality standards to a level of recognition in the education and training world similar to the consumer world's Good Housekeeping Seal of Approval and facilitate better decisions in selecting online courses.

Future Issues

MVU is continually striving to heighten its credibility and leadership in the education and training profession, addressing such issues as levels of technology available to students and workers; access for those with disabilities; and the demand for new content, particularly in IT modules where technology changes are frequent.

Because most of MVU's funding to date has been channeled through state grants, its objectives have been closely aligned with those of Michigan agencies and state departments. With the expectation that MVU will be financially self-sufficient by 2003, MVU may face difficult decisions in balancing revenue-producing programs and services with its public policy responsibilities.

Author's Note: My thanks to Deb White for her assistance with this case study.

INDEX